GUIDE TO
Implementing and Managing
Patron-Driven Acquisitions

ACQUISITIONS GUIDES SERIES

Guide to Video Acquisitions in Libraries: Issues and Best Practices, #15
Mary S. Laskowski, 60p. 2011, ALA
ISBN: 978-0-8389-8575-5

Writing RFPs for Acquisitions: A Guide to the Request for Proposal, #14
Frances C. Wilkinson and Linda K. Lewis, 84p. 2008, ALA.
ISBN: 978-0-8389-8483-3

Guide to Licensing and Acquiring Electronic Information, #13
Stephen Bosch et al., 112p. 2005, Scarecrow Press.
ISBN: 0-8108-5259-4

Guide to Out-of-Print Materials, #12
Narda Tafuri et al., 46p. 2004, Scarecrow Press.
ISBN: 0-8108-4132-0

Guide to Managing Approval Plans, #11
Susan Flood, 58p. 1998, ALA.
ISBN: 0-8389-3481-1

Guide to Performance Evaluation of Serials Vendors, #10
38p. 1997, ALA.
ISBN: 0-8389-3469-2

Guide to Selecting and Acquiring CD-ROMs, Software, and other Electronic Publications, #09
Stephen Bosch et al., 48p. 1994, ALA.
ISBN: 0-8389-0629-X

Guide to Preservation in Acquisition Processing, #08
Marsha J. Hamilton, 34p. 1993, ALA.
ISBN: 0-8389-0611-7

*Guidelines for Handling Library Orders for Serials
and Periodicals*, 2d ed., #07
19p. 1992, ALA.
ISBN: 0-8389-3416-1

Statistics for Managing Library Acquisitions, #06
Eileen D. Hardy, 11p. 1989, ALA
ISBN: 0-8389-3374-2

*Guide to Performace Evaluation of Library
Materials Vendors*, #05
20p. 1988, ALA.
ISBN: 0-8389-3369-6

*Guidelines for Handling Library Orders for In-Print
Monographic Publications*, 2d ed, #04
Sara C. Heitshu, 21p. 1984, ALA.
ISBN: 0-8389-3148-0

*Guidelines for Handling Library Orders
for Microforms*, #03
Harriet Rebuldela, 14p. 1977, ALA
ISBN: 0-8389-3193-6

*Guidelines for Handling Library Orders for Serials
and Periodicals*, #02
Murray S. Martin, 16p. 1974, ALA.
ISBN: 0-8389-3158-8

*Guidelines for Handling Library Orders for In-Print
Monographic Publications*, #01
Murray S. Martin, 10p. 1973, ALA.
ISBN: 0-8389-3148-0

ALCTS ACQUISITIONS GUIDES SERIES, NO. 16

GUIDE TO
Implementing and Managing
Patron-Driven
Acquisitions

SUZANNE M. WARD

Association for Library Collections
& Technical Services
American Library Association

Chicago   2012

Association for Library Collections & Technical Services (ALCTS)
is a division of the American Library Association

ALCTS Publishing
50 E. Huron St.
Chicago, IL 60611

www.ala.org/alcts

The paper used in this publication meets the minimum requirements of American
National Standard for Information Sciences—Permanence of Paper for Printed
Library Materials, ANSI Z39.48-1992.

Library of Congress Cataloging-in-Publication Data

Ward, Suzanne M.

  Guide to implementing and managing patron-driven acquisitions /
    Suzanne M. Ward.
      pages   cm. — (ALCTS acquisitions guides ; no. 16)
  Includes bibliographical references and index.
  ISBN 978-0-8389-8608-0 (alk. paper)
  1. Patron-driven acquisitions (Libraries) I. Title.
  Z689.W37 2012
  025.2—dc23   2012019007

ISBN-13: 978-0-8389-8608-0

Printed in the United States of America

16   15   14   13   12   5   4   3   2   1

contents

1

Overview *1*

Purpose *2*

Scope *3*

2

**Traditional Collection Development
and Interlibrary Loan** *5*

Traditional Interlibrary Loan Model *7*

Interlibrary Loan Book Purchase Model *8*

Buying Instead of Borrowing *11*

3

Starting a PDA Program *13*

Considerations for Print Book PDA through Interlibrary Loan *14*

Administration and Processing *17*

Beyond the Pilot Stage: Operations and Workflow *25*

4

PDA and E-books *27*

Types of E-book PDAs *28*

Setting Up an E-book PDA Program *31*

5

Alternatives to PDA *49*

Print Books through the OPAC *49*

Hybrid PDA Model: Print and Electronic *51*

Innovative Services *52*

6

Cons   *55*

Resource Sharing   *55*

Costs   *56*

Staff Time   *57*

Effects on the Collection   *58*

7

Future Directions   *61*

selected bibliography   *65*

reference notes   *71*

about the author   *77*

Figures

Figure 1.   Considerations for Choosing an E-book Aggregator   31

Figure 2.   Considerations for Evaluating an E-book Pilot Project   40

Figure 3.   Questions for Ongoing Assessment   45

1 Overview

Patron-driven acquisitions (PDA) refers to a formal plan or program where librarians develop criteria for selecting books that will be bought based on patrons' requests or use. In most models, the patrons do not know that their actions trigger purchases. In the traditional print-based model, librarians buy books requested through interlibrary loan (ILL) if they meet certain criteria.

A more recent print-based approach involves loading a book vendor's titles into the library catalog and letting patrons select the titles they need, often indicating how quickly they need the books. Electronic books offer a similar model: librarian-profiled e-book records are loaded into library catalogs and patron interactions with the e-books trigger purchases when certain thresholds have been met. Some libraries manage hybrid programs in which both print and electronic books are added based on patron use or request, depending on the point at which patrons request or use the titles, or based on patron preference.

The underlying premise behind the PDA concept is that a book that one patron finds useful now will likely appeal to other patrons in the future. Further, patron-selected books will enjoy greater overall use than librarian-selected ones. In all cases, library staff apply criteria concerning which books are eligible for addition to the collection and which are not.

What are the benefits of PDA? It adds books to the collection with a guarantee of at least one use and the promise of higher-than-average subsequent use. Users such as graduate students, who typically do not have an active role in collection development, find that their requests strengthen the collection in ways that benefit not only the original requestors, but also their peers. PDA often acquires titles so recently published that some of them would be impossible to obtain through ILL borrowing. It also provides a safety net for acquiring interdisciplinary works that might otherwise fall through the cracks of traditional collection development. Selectors assessing the purchased books at one academic library summarized the benefits by concluding that "on-demand acquisitions as a result of ILL book requests are a customer-centered, cost-effective, easy, and high-impact way to complement normal collection development."[1]

PURPOSE

This guide will help librarians decide whether a patron-driven acquisitions program will be beneficial for their users. If the answer is yes, the guide then prompts librarians through:

- determining criteria and workflow;
- setting up a pilot project;
- short- and long-term assessment strategies; and
- considering the integration of print-based PDA programs with emerging e-book options.

A chapter titled "Cons" explores some reasons why libraries might decide either not to engage in PDA programs or perhaps to wait until early implementers and vendors have gained enough experience to simplify, standardize, and streamline some of the practices.

PDA is a relatively new term. The concept started gaining significant attention in the early 2000s, when print was still king. Earlier terms included: buy not borrow, ILL book purchase program, books on demand, purchase on demand, demand-driven acquisitions, buy vs. borrow, patron-initiated collection development, and just-in-time acquisitions.

SCOPE

Users in many kinds of libraries can benefit from PDA programs, but most of the literature on PDA and on related topics such as circulation studies and interlibrary loan costs comes from the academic arena. Despite the fact that several successful ILL-based PDA programs are in public libraries, there are very few references in print to programs outside academe.[2] Only one article from a school library was found at the time of this publication.[3] The paucity of reports from nonacademic libraries means that most examples will be from college and university libraries, but the principles may be applied in other settings.

Because e-book PDA is still both a relatively new concept and an evolving one, few libraries have moved past the pilot phase and into PDA as standard operating procedure. The literature to date focuses mainly on ILL print-based programs and the results of e-book pilot projects conducted by early implementers.

This guide confines itself to books, both print and electronic. There are established and emerging models in the journal world wherein librarians consider moving from the subscription-based tradition to article-based purchases or acquisitions based on patron requests, but that discussion is beyond the scope of this book. This book also excludes the practice of occasionally buying material like dissertations or technical reports and giving them to patrons to keep, since this practice does not actually develop the collection. Even in cases where librarians acquire these gray literature titles and add them to the collection after patron use, the practice does not embrace the spirit of PDA, since these often esoteric titles generally have limited potential for further use by other patrons. Acquiring them may also involve a much more complicated workflow than the relatively straightforward approach of buying familiar publishers' titles from standard booksellers.

2 Traditional Collection Development and Interlibrary Loan

lmost by definition, a library's major responsibilities are acquiring, classifying, and providing access to the resources that its users need. Librarians strive to tailor the local collection specifically for their particular user population. A corporate law library collection is very different from that of a small liberal arts college because the users' needs are not the same. To build collections that meet their users' needs, librarians scour publishers' catalogs and set up elaborate profiles with book vendors. Some of them review interlibrary loan transactions looking for repeat requests for certain titles or for signs of emerging areas of study. They rely on their own subject expertise and knowledge of their local patrons' use patterns. They may read reviews or solicit suggestions from certain user groups, such as faculty.

Historically, librarians responded, usually positively, to users' suggestions for additions to the collection, although there is little documented evidence of this before patron-driven acquisitions programs began. Some requests arrive informally through a conversation at the reference desk or in a faculty member's office; others are more formally solicited through suggestion boxes or online request forms. In general, if patrons' requests match the library's collection policies and budget constraints, the items will be purchased. Until relatively recently, however, users' requests for the purchase of specific library materials constituted a very small percentage of most libraries' total acquisitions. Librarians felt confident that their choices were best for their collections and their users; interlibrary loan could be relied upon as a back-up to obtain those few, obscure items that patrons might occasionally need that did not match the library's primary collection focus. Examination of several classic collection development textbooks confirms that although the authors emphasize the importance of the librarian's role in collection development *for* the patron community, there is no mention of input in collection development *by* the patron community.

Confident that they were building collections that matched users' needs, librarians were astonished when reports began to appear, starting with Trueswell's often-cited 1969 article, that revealed that a relatively small percentage of a collection received most of the use and also that large percentages of collections were never used at all.[4] The advent of automated circulation systems made it possible to compile data for these studies, which were mainly reported by academic librarians.

Thus it became evident that over the years academic libraries spent huge sums on material that their users seldom or never used, yet which had been acquired after the librarians' careful consideration that these were items that their patrons would need. Borrowing from the terminology of the industrial world, academic libraries built huge "just in case" collections, but an alarmingly high percentage of books in them saw little or no use. Costs escalated beyond the initial purchase: low- and no-use books needed to be cataloged; shelved; inventoried; shifted; barcoded; and, finally, weeded or, more likely, identified for removal to off-campus storage facilities. In the 1960s and 1970s, book and construction budgets were often large and elastic and there seemed to be no pressing need to change the collection development model so long as funds and space permitted the addition of tens of thousands of new books each year.

TRADITIONAL INTERLIBRARY LOAN MODEL

Interlibrary loan (ILL) provided librarians with a safety net for borrowing the few items that the library did not hold—those long-tail titles like obscure foreign-language books or arcane technical reports that fell far outside the library's scope to acquire but which occasionally provide helpful supplementary information for scholars. "Long tail" refers to a concept introduced by Chris Anderson; for any given commodity (cereal to songs) most of the use or sales and therefore most of the profit will occur with a few items, and then there will be a long tail of many minor items that each have low or niche use, although collectively the long tail may represent a considerable market. Although a use or sale of any individual long tail item does not yield much profit, cumulatively the sales of many long tail items do.[5] Businesses like iTunes and Amazon.com thrive on this principle.

In the 1980s and 1990s, the access vs. ownership debate began as library budgets faced cutbacks in the midst of cost increases and an information explosion. Administrators sought to provide better access through resource sharing to materials that they could no longer afford to purchase. Librarians selected core or essential acquisitions, but interlibrary loan handled requests for supplementary material. ILL services certainly improved, aided by automation and stronger consortial agreements, but few addressed the core problem: a huge number of librarian-selected titles sat unused on shelves while requests for interlibrary loans mushroomed.[6] Kane summarizes the ownership access vs. ownership dilemma as it stood in the mid-1990s.[7]

It should also be noted that in some libraries such as smaller academic ones, faculty make most or all of the book selection decisions. This book is not the place to debate the pros or cons of this arrangement, but anecdotal evidence suggests that this model may not often be much better than the one in which librarian selectors make most of the decisions.[8] As just one example, the author recently heard a colleague from a small liberal arts college remark that faculty often submit orders for books of critical essays about works that the library does not own; she struggled to retain control over a small portion of the collection budget so that she could occasionally buy a few titles to fill gaps like these.

INTERLIBRARY LOAN BOOK PURCHASE MODEL

In an ideal world, librarians would anticipate and acquire most of the material that their patrons needed and interlibrary loan would fill in the gap by borrowing a few obscure titles. We do not live in that ideal world, however. No library holds everything its users might need. If a library's collection development practices are sound and its budget is relatively healthy, it will have many needed items, but certainly not all of them. There are many reasons for this gap:

- collection budgets shrink in difficult economic times;
- book costs rise at a higher percentage than collection budgets do;
- new formats emerge and the library acquire must acquire essential titles in more than one format until one emerges triumphant (e.g., VHS vs. Betamax) or supplants its predecessor (e.g., DVD vs. VHS);
- users' needs and preferences for formats vary (e.g., large print vs. regular edition vs. e-book vs. book on CD vs. children's abridgement or adaptation);
- new areas of study or interest emerge;
- purchasing more than a tiny fraction of the huge annual output of titles on certain topics (e.g., computer programming) is very difficult; and
- titles are updated and reissued annually (e.g., test and tax preparation books).

Although documentation is scarce, a large portion of interlibrary loan requests are not for obscure technical reports and works in foreign languages. ILL serves as a library's safety net for obtaining many of those kinds of materials, but each year ILL is also heavily used for borrowing hundreds or thousands of titles that are relatively recently published books on topics that match the library's core collection development areas, but which were not identified or selected for purchase. Roberts and Cameron found that more than half of the ILL books requested by their library's patrons had been published in the previous six years. They observed that "the overwhelming preponderance of recently published material was obvious." They further noted that "these were frequently low-priced and purchaseable [in print]" and concluded that "some of this could and should be bought either instead of, or in addition to, borrowing."[9]

Librarians have long known that examination of past interlibrary loan transactions can provide clues to weak areas of the collection and can even suggest specific books to buy.[10] However, prior to ILL automation and the development of spreadsheets, reviewing and analyzing transactions was a laborious process usually involving sorting through piles of paper request slips. Should one sort by title? By patrons' academic departments? Assign and then sort by call number or general subject areas? The first automation efforts did not help the process much, since in the early days ILL transactions were only computerized while they were "live;" completed transactions usually dropped off the system or could not captured locally. Sometimes printed reports were available, but it was not always possible to select the data elements needed for collection analysis or to sort the results in a meaningful way.

Over the past few decades, several authors reported on their reviews of ILL book loan transactions (sometimes correlated with circulation studies and collection size) and summarized their conclusions. While all were motivated by wanting to provide better services for their users, some of them were looking for a cheaper alternative to interlibrary loan while others focused on collection building. Over this time span many things changed, such as the average cost of ILL transactions, the average cost of books, workflow standards, automation, and even the transition of interlibrary loan itself from an auxiliary to a core service, but still librarians grappled with the challenge of trying to figure out why they were borrowing books, sometimes multiple times, that would often have been good additions to their collections. The reviews and studies varied from the easy (and probably oversimplified) to the extremely complex (and thus unlikely to be carried out very often). Most studies also suffered from the drawback that specific findings at one library could not be generalized to other collections.

From reading the literature, it is also not clear just how many collection development librarians actually used the data on an ongoing basis to analyze their collections and buy titles to strengthen weak areas. In addition, relying on past ILL transactions to suggest future purchases meant that the library paid for a book at least twice: once to borrow it, and later to purchase it after reviewing the ILL logs.

In 1980 Pritchard described a study conducted on some ILL book loan requests from a medical library in the mid-1970s. The ILL staff there drew selected titles to the attention of the acquisitions staff and some of those titles were purchased instead of borrowed. Results showed that these books were recently published and that they circulated slightly better over a three-year period than had similar librarian-selected titles. Pritchard concluded that "it had not been foreseen that requests for books on interlibrary loan might, in fact, represent a continuing need for access to these books presumably from other library members in addition to the requestor" and recommended that "more weight be given in the future to this category of request in the Library's acquisition policy."[11]

An early article advocating this approach went so far as to recommend the then-revolutionary idea of buying books that cost as much as or less than an average ILL transaction.[12] In this example, staff at a regional public library system assessed the process by tracking the subsequent usage of books purchased in response to ILL requests as well as of a control selection of similar books. In follow-up assessment, Swanson found that most of these purchased books were subsequently used multiple times.

In 1988 another librarian weighed the philosophical pros and cons of borrowing books over purchasing them, but identified "serious problems in practice" because it would be impossible to predict "which books would or would not be used," stopping short of taking the next step of postulating that patrons' choices of books requested through ILL might, after profiling against librarian-developed selection criteria, be books with a high likelihood of subsequent use.[13]

Herslow-Fex's 1989 article described Lund University's practice of treating ILL requests for recent literature as a "suggested purchase" and stated her opinion that university library collections "should be developed mainly on the basis of . . . need . . . .There is no more useful instrument than the interlibrary loan requests from your local users."[14]

In 1996 Miller advocated a closer relationship between interlibrary loan and collection development, suggesting that "when items cannot be acquired by ILL, requests should go to collection management for a decision whether to purchase."[15]

Murphy and Rupp-Serrano suggested that "titles requested more than once could automatically generate an order for purchase. Requests for titles from the current publication year could also be flagged for automatic purchase."[16]

Bucknell University was another early implementer. In a 1999 article Perdue and Van Fleet discussed their efforts, beginning in 1990, to buy some of the books that ILL patrons requested. They assessed their efforts as successful, citing an acceptable turnaround time, reasonable average costs, inter-unit cooperation with acquisitions, and a high subsequent circulation rate.[17] This author considers the Bucknell service to be the first planned, criteria-driven, comprehensive, and sustained ILL PDA program documented in the literature, all the more remarkable because it started before the internet made instant access to online booksellers' sites an easy way to determine availability, cost, and expected delivery times.

BUYING INSTEAD OF BORROWING

With the advent of ILL management software, librarians could capture, maintain, and examine a wealth of information about past transactions, sort them in various ways, and export them to programs like Excel and Access for further manipulation and review.[18]

Analyzing ILL data is a laudable activity for many reasons, but whether alphabetizing paper slips or sorting fields in a database, the data represent past transactions. The library staff has already expended time, effort, and money in borrowing the books. In some cases the same titles have been obtained multiple times, either for the same patron or for different ones. Reviewing ILL transactions and then purchasing selected titles found there responds to potential future need, but occurs after the fact for the initial borrower(s) and results in multiple costs for the same title (borrowing first, and then buying).

The Association of Research Libraries (ARL) conducted one of its periodic in-depth studies of interlibrary loan costs in 1995 and published the results in 1998. The study found that for academic libraries the cost per filled ILL transaction was $18.35 for the borrowing library and $9.48 for the lending library, an average total of $27.83.[19]

In the late 1990s the twin events of this highly publicized average cost of nearly $30 per academic ILL transaction and the availability of an online bookseller (Amazon.com went online in 1995) independently suggested to several ILL librarians that some subset of ILL loan requests could be considered for immediate purchase rather than for traditional borrowing transactions. Not only was it now easy to determine which titles were immediately available and at what price, but delivery times also closely matched those of borrowed books. If the purchase criteria were crafted carefully, in theory the library would be buying books that not only satisfied one patron's immediate need, but also, the librarians theorized, had a reasonably high likelihood that, once added to the collection, would also meet future users' needs. What constituted that subset of ILL book requests? In general, obscure, highly specialized, foreign language, or out-of-print titles were not considered. Removing these books still left a large potential pool of relatively recently published titles likely to appeal to a readership beyond the requesting patron. Librarians developed selection criteria that were quick and easy to apply to loan requests.

In most cases the impetus of the early pilot projects was not saving money, or at least not primarily so. While it is true that a $10 purchase saves a $15 borrowing fee, most books meeting the selection criteria will cost far more than the average borrowing fee, not to mention the future costs of cataloging, shelving, and maintaining them. The reason for establishing ILL buying programs focused largely on exploring new ways of filling the requesting patrons' needs quickly while making the books readily available to future users; in other words, expanding collection development in a systematic and programmatic way based on patrons' expressed needs.

Early implementers who described their pilot projects in the literature were from Purdue University, the University of Wisconsin at Madison, and the Thomas Crane Public Library.[20]

3 Starting a PDA Program

In the early 2000s when most early implementers started their patron-initiated collection development programs through interlibrary loan, print books were the only option. While a few e-books were available, the vast majority of titles were only available in print; librarians had not yet started making conscious decisions to collect e-books systematically or aggressively.

Today, e-book PDA and print PDA options exist outside interlibrary loan. Libraries collect, and patrons often still want, a choice or mixture of print and electronic books. Librarians getting started in PDA might decide to establish a successful process with print books through interlibrary loan before adding an e-book component, or they might decide to focus on e-book PDA in the belief that even though not all titles are available electronically at the point of need, this format is the one for the future. Certainly both print and e-book programs can be run simultaneously, although in taking this approach librarians should make an effort to integrate them not only to prevent unnecessary duplication, but also to provide the best service mix for users.

All librarians starting these programs have the same questions to answer, although many of them develop different answers depending on local preferences and constraints.

CONSIDERATIONS FOR PRINT BOOK PDA THROUGH INTERLIBRARY LOAN

To begin a print book PDA program developed with patrons' ILL requests, first answer questions about establishing the purchase criteria: under what circumstances and how will the library buy rather than borrow a book on an interlibrary loan request form submitted by a patron?

Timing

Most libraries with an ILL book purchase program apply the criteria to all incoming loan requests from local patrons. However, a few apply the criteria only to requests that have either failed to be filled as loans from the first string of potential lenders, typically five libraries, or for which there are no potential lenders at all, possibly because of a very recent publication date or because they are esoteric, gray literature titles.[21] Delaying potential purchase decisions until a request has failed through interlibrary loan has the virtue of being a lesser strain on the budget and on staff time since lending partners fill most ILL loan requests. A disadvantage is that the request will have already aged several days through the normal process and then, having failed, will enter a second process that takes about a week. In addition, such a practice is less likely to add a significant number of books to the local collection.[22]

Maximum Cost

Setting the maximum cost too low in an effort to conserve program funds means that many potentially useful books will not be purchased. At Purdue University, the author proposed an initial cap of $50 in 1999, but raised it to $100 at the start of the pilot project in 2000 after a science librarian pointed out that few science or technology books could be acquired for $50 or less. A few years later, hoping to increase the number of sci/tech books added through the program, the cap was increased to $150. In practice, however, relatively few books cost more than $100 if they are in online booksellers' warehouses ready for immediate shipment; the average cost, including shipping fees, settled in the $40-50 range and has remained there for years. Librarians at a science and engineering library decided not to set a maximum cost at all because books in those disciplines tended to be expensive.[23] At the other end of the spectrum, librarians at an academic law library set $20 as the limit for ILL-based decision making in a conscious effort to buy some items more cheaply than the total loan cost (loan fee, processing costs, return shipping), although requests for books costing more than that amount were forwarded to the collection development department for purchase decisions.[24]

Publication Date

Librarians prefer to add only recently published books to the collection via patron-initiated purchases. Depending on the budget and how far it is likely to go based on other criteria, librarians usually decide on publication dates within two to five years of the current year. This practice has the advantage of ease and speed since most titles can be ordered quickly and easily from online booksellers or from other familiar sources. However, some librarians have explored buying out-of-print titles as well, checking web sites that list used books from thousands of booksellers. One public library director praised these bookstores for "reasonable prices and prompt delivery" when ILL proved "way too slow," although librarians evaluate each title after patron use to determine if it will be "sold, discarded, or added to the collection." Since the titles that his library's patrons needed were relatively inexpensive, he found it far more cost effective to buy them than to borrow them.[25] When librarians at a science and engineering library decided to eliminate publication date limits, they discovered that about 90 percent of the books purchased from ILL requests had been published within the most recent twenty years.[26]

Treatment

Academic librarians might make the decision that a book must be scholarly to be purchased, a factor that is open to some interpretation. However, if the same staff member makes most of the determinations, then the decisions will be consistent. At a public library, however, staff would want to buy many books that might not be considered scholarly, yet clearly meet user needs and conform to the collection policy. Academic librarians might consciously decide to exclude fiction, drama, or poetry, although they would buy literary criticism.

Format

Is there a preference for paperback editions when available? Paperbacks are of course less expensive, but are also less durable. Following the usual acquisitions guidelines on this point may be helpful.

Another format decision involves audio-visual media. Once past the pilot phase, librarians should consider adding media titles that otherwise meet the library's PDA criteria. For example, academic librarians might not buy a DVD of a recent blockbuster movie, but they might buy documentaries, foreign films, or classic movies that support the curriculum. Public librarians might be more inclined to buy popular movies, but possibly not many obscure, subtitled foreign films. What about sound recordings or books on CD? Once again, general collection development policies can provide guidance here.

Are textbooks (e.g., *Introduction to Accounting*, 5th edition) eligible? What are the interlibrary loan and collection development policies about textbooks? Would buying textbooks at patrons' requests take up too large a percent of the budget to the exclusion of adding other titles? What about textbook solution manuals?

What about other categories of books? A college library might not include juvenile literature in its PDA plan, but a public library might. What about test- or tax-preparation books that appear in new editions every year? Adding selected test-preparation, career-aid, or self-help books might be part of the library's regular collection development practice, but not part of the PDA plan. The staff member who applies the purchase criteria to the ILL book loan requests also needs to apply some common sense. For example, at the Purdue University Libraries, a faculty member once requested a large number of recently published, expensive art books. Because the university's art program is very small, the supervisor advised the selecting staff member to buy the books about major artists, but to borrow the ones about less-famous ones.

Language

English only? Or also other frequently-spoken local languages? If non-English titles are eligible, can the library obtain them as quickly as English-language books?

Ownership

Only titles not already held by the library are usually considered for purchase through the PDA plan. The PDA funds are not expected to cover second copies, but librarians should decide whether the program will buy books to replace officially missing ones based on a patron's request.

Patron Status

Are book requests from all patron groups eligible for purchase if they meet the criteria, or are there good local reasons for some restrictions? At the Brigham Young University library, for example, the book purchasing service through interlibrary loan requests was available only for faculty.[27]

Once you finalize your criteria, printing the list in easy-to-read bullet points may be useful. Are these points easily understandable? Will the ILL staff member who applies these criteria to incoming loan requests be able to do so quickly? Can the main points of the criteria be summarized easily in one sentence if necessary, such as "Recently published scholarly books in English that will be delivered within one week and that cost $100 or less?" Finally, determine the best ways to inform library administrators and collection development or acquisitions librarians about the criteria and involve them in the pilot or program.

ADMINISTRATION AND PROCESSING

Once the criteria are set, consider administrative and processing factors.

Length of Pilot

Ideally, the pilot project should last between six months and a year to allow enough time to buy enough books to have a large enough data set for meaningful evaluation, but librarians can also learn a lot from a shorter pilot if initial funding is limited. Remember that the shorter the pilot, the more difficult it is to gather relevant subsequent use data because not enough time will have passed to yield meaningful results.

Who Makes Purchase Decisions?

The requests arrive in interlibrary loan and, in many libraries, are handled by staff who are not librarians. An experienced ILL staffer can make purchase decisions based on clear criteria and after initial consultation with a librarian or supervisor for the first few days. A librarian who periodically reviews lists of the purchased titles can easily provide any necessary guidance to correct any decision making that might be going slightly awry.

In reviewing ten years' worth of purchased titles generated by ILL requests, Purdue selectors found that only about one percent of the books were ones that they would not have bought for the collection, and these tended to be self-help books (e.g., diet, pop psychology) and get-rich-quick books.[28] That comes to 100 books over a decade when nearly 10,000 books were purchased; 10 per year, a tiny number.

Some programs require that a librarian make purchase decisions based on the requests screened by staff. If the librarian is the head of interlibrary loan or acquisitions and is available on a nearly daily basis to make these decisions, the program should run smoothly. However, if the ILL assistant is expected to deal out the requests to dozens of subject specialists and wait for their responses before proceeding with either a book order or an ILL loan request, it is almost certain that the program will be less successful. It will be far more time consuming to wait for responses and to follow up on nonresponses from many other people, and the overall ILL turnaround time will suffer.

Who Places the Order?

Should the ILL staff place orders directly through the online bookseller or library book vendor? It is certainly very easy to do, but it may be prudent to send the requests to acquisitions for official ordering. Some institutions consider it good fiscal practice for the person placing the order and the person approving or handling the payment process to be different. In addition, if acquisitions staff place the orders, then titles enter the normal processing routine so that, among other things, "on order" records enter the catalog quickly so that other selectors do not inadvertently order duplicates.

Establish the workflow so that orders travel quickly to acquisitions so that staff can handle these time-sensitive orders accordingly.

Delivery Time

Buying rather than borrowing books based on interlibrary loan requests works best when the delivery time for a purchased book is comparable to that of a loaned book. For most libraries, that time interval is about a week (five business days). Can the person placing the orders tell when a particular book will be shipped or delivered? Online booksellers' web sites often indicate in-stock information and expected shipment or delivery times, along with the price. If a library book vendor's site offers in-stock and price information, is it dependable for shipping books for arrival within about a week?

When to Catalog?

Where should the book be sent? Should it be delivered to technical services for cataloging first? If so, should it then be lent from a circulation desk or sent to interlibrary loan to be lent as an ILL book? Do technical services staff understand the time factor with these books, and are they willing to rush catalog them? Are they willing and able to rush catalog all the books expected to be purchased through the program? At Purdue, with about a thousand books ordered each year as a result of ILL requests, it was not practical to expect the cataloging staff to handle so many books on a rush basis. Books purchased as a result of ILL requests are delivered directly to the ILL office where the staff add a property stamp and then treat the books exactly like any other ILL loan. The books are cataloged after patron use. However, the cataloging staff are happy to expedite those books when the ILL patron, having exhausted the maximum number of ILL renewals, would like the book rush-cataloged so he or she can check it out for the longer local circulation loan period.

The author has heard of some instances in which libraries with ILL print PDA programs place the books on a shelf or cart after patron use so that the selectors can review and make the final retention decision. This practice might be useful during the pilot phase as one way to check that the books meet the purchase criteria, but should be unnecessary thereafter. If the criteria are sound and their application consistent, almost all of the purchased books will be useful additions to the collection.

Books' Final Destination

Who decides where the books will finally reside after the ILL patron's initial use? At Purdue, the staff member who determines which books meet the purchasing criteria also designates the campus library that will eventually receive the book after it is cataloged. She makes the decision based largely on the subject covered by the book itself, although sometimes the patron's departmental affiliation comes into play. Even though librarians may later decide that a few books really belong in another location, it is faster and cheaper to catalog the books for a designated location and then make a few changes a year if needed. The ultimate destination is noted in the ILL-management software; later analysis can be made in part on patrons' departments and books' final homes, thus highlighting interdisciplinary interest.[29]

Choosing Suppliers

When ILL PDA started, credit card use was new in many libraries. Librarians in at least one library initially had to limit their suppliers to those that would accept OCLC's ILL Fee Management (IFM) payment service, thus restricting most purchases to titles available through a used book aggregator that listed its holdings in the OCLC database.[30] Using credit cards has now become standard practice in most libraries, so it is easy to take advantage of the ease of ordering and speed of delivery associated with online booksellers. In most print-based PDA programs, the acquisitions staff place the orders based on title selection by ILL staff. It makes sense to use the same suppliers that are usually preferred for a combination of good prices coupled with quick and reliable service for expedited orders.

While most libraries engaged in ILL book purchase PDA programs buy new books and add them to the collection, some librarians have contemplated the often very low cost of buying a used copy of older imprints from online used book sellers. One library sampled one hundred ILL requests and discovered that nearly 80 percent could have been purchased rather than borrowed, one third of them for less than $10 and some for less than $5.[31] Filling patrons' requests by buying books this way would be far cheaper than traditional borrowing; some of the titles could be sent to the library book sale or discarded after the patron's use if they were not needed for the collection, thus saving cataloging and future maintenance costs. Depending on the PDA criteria and budget, it is possible to use dealers listed with the out-of-print online book sites at least some of the time.

Identify Exceptions

Criteria and policies cover the vast majority of instances, but what kinds of possible exceptions might staff encounter? One example might be a book that costs just over the maximum cost limit but, because it was so recently published, is unlikely to be available from ILL lending partners. Another example would be a low-priced book published in another country or language that is available from an international online bookseller for less than the cost of an international loan, taking return airmail shipping costs into consideration. Who makes decisions about exceptions—the staff member who typically applies the criteria to the ILL loan requests or a supervisor?

Set up Tracking

It is important to add some kind of tag to records for books acquired through the ILL purchase program so that it is easy to identify them when compiling statistics and conducting assessments. This tagging may be done in one or both of two places; first, the interlibrary loan management program and second, by fund code in the acquisitions module of the library's integrated library system (ILS). For the ILL management system, it will probably be necessary to establish a library or vendor code for this purpose, and then the transactions can be handled as any other loans, with the possibility of querying the system later for aggregate information about the number of books acquired, patron categories, turnaround time, average price and other details. While some of this information might be duplicated in both places (e.g., price, number of books), additional critical information can be gathered from each of the systems, such as subsequent circulation from the ILS and patrons' departmental affiliation from the ILL management system.

Staff Roles and Interaction

Interlibrary loan and acquisitions staff may not have worked together much in the past. Does everyone understand the essential steps of everyone's job in this new workflow? Does everyone know who to ask if there is a problem or a bottleneck? Are the supervisors of the two units coordinating their efforts to assess workflow effectiveness and efficiency? Who are the back-up staff members in both ILL and acquisitions? Identifying and correcting problems quickly is vital to avoid delaying patrons' requests.

Troubleshooting

A few glitches are inevitable, but there are typically no more than with the usual ILL and acquisitions workflow. Checking once a week to see if any orders are languishing unfilled after ten or fourteen days is helpful. These orders should be cancelled and moved straight to an ILL transaction.

Plan Assessment

Before starting the pilot project, be clear about what factors will be assessed to determine the program's level of success, and then be sure that data about those factors are captured during transaction processing and can be readily queried. Remember that although the data support the assessment, data alone will probably not be sufficient for an administrator. Some tables and statistics are helpful, but the assessment report should include summaries, conclusions, and recommendations as well. The author evaluated her library's pilot program in four areas:

- patron feedback;
- staff perceptions;
- analysis of the pilot project data; and
- administrators' perceptions.[32]

Data to gather include the number of books purchased; total cost for each book (including shipping cost); basic bibliographic information (author, title, publisher, publication date); and order date and date of receipt to determine turnaround time. Librarians at college and university libraries will probably also want to track patron status (faculty, staff, graduate student, undergraduate student) and academic department, as well as the branch library that eventually shelves the cataloged book.

Subsequent use information is an important measure of a PDA program's success, but during a pilot project, even one of a year's duration, there is not enough time for books to circulate a meaningful number of times past the requesting patron's use. Published in-depth subsequent use studies for ILL purchase-on-demand books examined use over long periods: ten years at Purdue University and five years at the University of Nebraska-Lincoln.[33] Preliminary figures can be reported, however, since these often demonstrate a promising beginning.[34]

Foss describes a bookmark inserted into each PDA volume that asked, among other things, if patrons wanted to check the book out again once it has been cataloged after their ILL use. During the pilot program, 74 percent of patrons responded yes, triggering rush cataloging so the book can be checked out again for the library's normal loan period.[35] Hussong-Christian and Goergen-Doll report similarly high intended subsequent use indicated by patrons: 56 percent said "yes" and 35 percent said "maybe."[36]

Also, while administrators may be particularly interested in supporting statistics early in a program's life, after the program has established itself, the program manager should prepare and report statistics on at least an annual basis. Be sure to include patron feedback in the early reports.

Gathering Patron Feedback

Gathering patron feedback on the pilot program can be a challenge when, in general, the program purposely receives no publicity and patrons have no idea when they submit ILL book loan requests that some of the titles might be purchased instead of borrowed. At Purdue, the author solved this challenge by developing colored paper slips to insert into each purchased book with a brief printed explanation of the project and a two-question survey: had the book arrived in good time and did the patron rate the book as very useful, moderately useful, or marginally useful as an addition to the library collection? There was also an area for comments. Patrons returned the survey slips with many of the purchased books and staff compiled the results periodically. Patrons reported that the books almost always arrived in good time and most rated the books as very useful to the collection. Most written comments also praised the program or the book.[37] Once the program had proved its worth and became part of routine operations, the ILL staff used smaller colored slips with a brief explanation about why the book had been purchased instead of borrowed, and discontinued the survey questions.

Hussong-Christian and Goergen-Doll describe the results of collecting feedback from their customers during a year-long ILL book purchase pilot.[38]

Facilitate Interaction with Subject Specialists

Some selectors express a concern that books in their areas of expertise are being bought by interlibrary loan staff, even though the purchasing only occurs when prompted by a patron's request. At one library, "subject specialists expressed a desire to be notified immediately of any title added to their collection."[39] While title-by-title notification may be too time-consuming in a large operation, it may be helpful early in the process to provide quarterly lists so that the selectors can review the kinds of materials being purchased. These lists can be easily generated from the ILL or ILS systems if each purchase was tagged in some way, such as with a special fund code, to identify it as a PDA title. Together with some background reading of in-depth and positive assessments of other programs, these periodic lists should allay selectors' fears that "unworthy" titles might be entering the collection.[40]

Set the Budget

Last, but certainly not least, consider the budget allocation for the program. The first step should be to estimate approximately how much the library would need to spend to buy all the books that meet the criteria. One way to do this is to review ILL loan transactions from a recent six- or twelve-month period or, in an academic library, from a recent semester. Several authors explain different approaches to making this estimate.[41] Such a study provides information not only an approximate budget estimate for a six- or twelve-month pilot project, but also provides a list of the kinds of books that meet the purchase criteria.

Can sufficient funds can be allocated to cover the anticipated cost? If not, the two choices are to revise the criteria and recalculate the estimates until the available funds and the estimated costs are approximately equal, or to understand that using the preferred criteria will exhaust the funds before they can be replenished in the next budget cycle.

Where will the funds come from? Can the regular collection development budget support the project? Can it do so without reducing money from allocations normally made to departments, subjects, or branch libraries (a potentially unpopular move before the program has proved itself)? Are there some discretionary, gift, or one-time funds available for the pilot project? Ruppel suggests using the replacement fund for lost books for the pilot project.[42]

At Purdue, the author was extraordinarily lucky in that the collection development officer fully funded the program from the pilot phase onwards with nonrecurring funds for the first few years. No traditional budget lines were reduced to pay for the new program, and sufficient funds were available, and regularly replenished, to buy all the books that met the purchase criteria. By the time that the monograph budget contracted about 2008, most selectors understood the important role that the patron-selected Books on Demand program played in adding useful books to the collection; funding the ILL book purchase plan from then on from regular monograph funds did not cause much dismay. Librarians at the University of Wisconsin-Madison started the pilot project with funds from the collection development budget, but shifted to using gift funds when the program moved into general practice.[43]

BEYOND THE PILOT STAGE: OPERATIONS AND WORKFLOW

Most ILL PDA programs reported in the literature have been successful. In at least one case, the first attempt was not a success, but several years later a second effort with an adjusted workflow provided better results.[44] Some successful pilot programs stumble over the obstacle of sustainable funding.

After a pilot program has been deemed successful in that it demonstrates that it fulfills the goals of adding useful material to the collection, the next stage is to operationalize it into standard practice. Most workflow issues should have been solved during the pilot phase, but if not, these can now be addressed or modified.

Formats
Decide if any other material formats, such as CDs or DVDs, should be added to the criteria. If so, remember to adjust the budget accordingly if initial estimates were made for books only.

Funding
If one-time or specially earmarked funds were used for the pilot, administrators need to identify funds to use on an ongoing basis. It may be difficult at first to consider allocating funds from the general collection development

budget, thus potentially reducing the amount available for traditional collection development. However, the analysis of the local pilot project combined with the overwhelming positive results reported in the literature, provide strong reasons for continuing to build part of the collection based on patron requests, even if means less support for traditional collection building.

Ongoing Assessment

At intervals, the ILL manager should provide interested parties with summaries such as the average cost per book, the average number of books per patron, the average turnaround time as compared with normal ILL loans, the percentage of purchased books vs. borrowed books, number of books by broad subject areas, and so on. In the program's early days, selectors and administrators may be interested in each semester's activity; later, cumulative annual data may be sufficient. Determine what colleagues want to know about the program, and then capture and supply that data periodically.

Also look for outliers that might affect averages; are there valid reasons for pulling these out and reporting them separately? For example, Brug and MacWaters note delivery times between three and 24 days with an average of 7.48 days. A small number of titles from foreign, society, or out-of-print dealers took much longer for delivery than those arriving from online bookseller.[45] In cases like these, it might be useful to separate or annotate the small number of exceptions and focus on the fact that most transactions met expectations.

After a successful pilot project of buying print books based on patrons' ILL requests, librarians may want to consider moving into the e-book PDA arena to supplement the ILL print PDA program.

4 PDA and E-books

Electronic books with their 24/7 access and extra features are here to stay. Most libraries currently sit somewhere on the continuum between having dabbled in buying a few e-books and having enthusiastically embraced them. While e-books have many virtues, they also pose many challenges. In compiling their SPEC kit on e-book collections for the Association for Research Libraries, Anson and Connell summed up the current situation: "The survey captures strong enthusiasm for e-books tempered by frustration with publisher policies, staff resistance to a changing model, and confusion over multiple interfaces and platform access."[46] However, this book is not the place to enumerate the many pros, cons, and issues associated with e-books; for helpful overviews, read the article "Resolving the Challenge of E-Books" or the essays in *No Shelf Required: E-Books in Libraries* and *No Shelf Required 2: Use and Management of E-Books.*[47] As with any radical new model, early implementation brings with it a bumpy ride. Time will solve most of the challenges as publishers, librarians, and patrons reach consensus on the arrangements that best suit all parties.

One major dilemma now facing librarians is the need to make a conscious decision about whether books should be duplicated in both print and electronic versions in some cases, or if there is a preference for one format over the other in cases where both versions exist. Some duplication is inevitable. For example, if a library buys a publisher's backlist e-book package, it may at least partially duplicate existing print copies. However, when faced with a choice of a traditional print title and its equivalent (and potentially more expensive) electronic twin, which one does the librarian choose? Each library's answer will be based on local preferences and constraints, and each library's answer may change over the next few years. Pitcher and her colleagues describe a requesting system in which patrons indicate their format preference.[48]

TYPES OF E-BOOK PDAS

Patron-driven acquisitions, which works so well in a print environment with ILL requests, can be adapted and broadened in the e-book arena. Polanka summarizes the benefits of e-book PDA as "guaranteed usage of new titles and proven usage of purchased titles, automatic acquisition, and seamless access for patrons. In addition, PDA can save time and eliminate guesswork for selectors, and it can be a cost-effective alternative to ILL."[49] Librarians can acquire e-books in four major ways: title-by-title selection; subscription e-book plan; purchasing e-book packages; and setting up an e-book PDA program.

Many librarians combine some or all of these activities in an effort to bring their patrons a variety of titles that best match their needs at reasonable prices.

Title-by-Title Selection. Library book vendors offer many titles in e-book format, often from more than one e-book aggregator. Selectors can easily see when e-book versions are available and can buy them from the vendor as easily as they can a print book. Technical processing staff then import the MARC records into the library's online public access catalog (OPAC), where the links provide patrons with immediate access to the e-books. Prices range from equal to the print version to significantly more. Some publishers issue e-books at the same time as the printed volume;

others wait until months later. Many e-books are also available for individual purchase directly from the publisher or issuing organization. Librarians may select individual e-books during routine collection development, or if they are available, e-books can be purchased one at a time in response to patrons' ILL requests (see Hybrid PDA Model). Selected open access e-book titles can also be cataloged and added to a catalog.

Subscription E-Book Plans. Some e-book aggregators offer subscription e-books plans that libraries or consortia often find attractive. For an annual fee (that usually varies based on the number of customers at each library's location), librarians add thousands of e-book records to their catalogs. The cost per title is usually very low, and there are typically no fees beyond the annual subscription fee and possibly a hosting or access fee; there will not be additional charges based on the number of times patrons access each title, for example. Librarians should be aware of the drawbacks, however. The pool of e-books may not include recently published titles. The vendor may remove titles at any time. A variation of this model allows the library to buy access to a certain number of books from the vendor's e-book list; the selectors have control over what titles they add or drop, but they must remain within the limit of the number of books allowed in the subscription agreement, or pay additional fees for more titles. If the library does not renew the subscription, it of course loses access to all those titles. The patron-driven aspect of this approach is that librarians can review usage reports to identify the most heavily used titles, and then consider buying them separately, even though they are in essence paying a second time for those titles. Libraries with tight budgets may find that this solution for gaining access to thousands of e-book titles is the only one possible.

Purchasing E-Book Packages. Libraries or consortia can also choose to purchase publishers' e-book packages. These are offered in a variety of ways, such as all the titles published in a certain date range or all titles in a particular subject collection. Backlists become available over time and there is of course the question of paying for each year's new titles, usually in advance. Aggregators also sell several varieties of e-book packages. The library usually buys perpetual access to the titles. There is no user-driven element in these purchases. Librarians make the best choices possible; as with print collections, patrons use a few titles heavily, some occasionally, and many not at all. The package deals price the cost per book low enough to be attractive when compared to buying selected titles individually. There arc also in-house savings when handling one invoice, one batch of records, etc. versus the higher per-title cost for single purchases. The downside is the fact that lower costs notwithstanding, patrons will not use many of the titles in these bundles.

E-Book PDA Program. Even at this early stage in their development, e-books have established their place in patron-driven acquisitions. Some librarians who never adopted the print book model as part of interlibrary loan operations now experiment with e-book PDA programs. Other librarians with years of experience with the ILL request print model now wonder whether to switch or wonder how or whether to integrate both formats.

A few years ago, librarians worked directly with e-book aggregators to set up their e-book PDA programs. In the very early stages of developing this concept, librarians faced title lists of tens of thousands of books and struggled to reduce these lists to a manageable number of relevant titles for their institutions. Deduplication with the existing collection was slow and difficult. Once the records had been loaded into the catalog, a user's single click triggered the purchase. Apocryphal stories circulated about tens of thousands of dollars being spent on e-book PDA pilot programs within a few weeks. Both librarians and vendors realized that the concept needed to be fine-tuned before many libraries would adopt it. Developing the profile and reviewing the title lists needed to be much easier, and there needed to be more options besides an instant purchase the moment a user opened a record.

By late 2010, several major aggregators had integrated their PDA operations with the same library book vendors with which they already offered e-books for title-by-title purchase. This integration meant that librarians could work with their established book vendor and build a customized e-book PDA plan around profiles that they had already developed. After finalizing the e-book PDA profile, the records for e-books that match the profile are entered into the library's OPAC where they look nearly or exactly identical to the e-book records for titles that the library already owns or subscribes to. In the course of their research, patrons encounter these records and access the full text just as they would any other e-book. After meeting some predetermined threshold of browsing, printing, downloading, or reading, patron use triggers either a rental fee or an outright purchase. Most libraries start with a trial period and assess those results before embarking on a larger, permanent program.

SETTING UP AN E-BOOK PDA PROGRAM

Setting up an e-book PDA program requires answering many of the same questions asked when establishing an ILL purchase program, but also introduces some new ones.

Choosing an E-Book Aggregator

There are several e-book aggregators. The author purposely chose not to mention vendors by name. The players change over time; their programs, features, and partnerships also change. They all have different title lists (with some overlap); different rental/purchase models; and different platforms. They have begun integrating their holdings with large library vendors to take advantage of the book profiling that has already been done for the vendors' customers.

Scheduling a webinar with each vendor gives librarians a feel for each product and offers a chance to ask questions. Many points to consider are listed in figure 1.

FIGURE 1

Considerations for Choosing an E-Book Aggregator

CONTENT/COSTS

What is the approximate overlap of titles between the aggregators under consideration or, to look at it another way, which aggregator has the largest number of unique titles?

What is the depth of the aggregator's backlist? Does it add to the backlist, focus on new titles, or both?

Are the major subject areas that support the library's user community represented adequately?

How many titles does the vendor have now, and approximately how many are added each year?

What are the options and cost differences for single user access and multiple user access?

If the aggregator uses a rental model, where is the usual or average cost/benefit point: in other words, after how many uses is it generally more cost effective to buy the book than to continuing to pay for each use?

If the library already holds a number of e-books on a title-by-title basis, is one of the aggregators clearly leading in terms of the number of e-books purchased and, if so, is that sufficient reason to prefer that aggregator on the grounds that it appears to carry the most titles that the library's users might need?

LICENSE TERMS

Ask to review a copy of the license; does it allow interlibrary loan for chapters within the constraints of the copyright law? What about provisions for using books or chapters for e-reserves?

What provisions have been made for the library's perpetual access to the titles that it has purchased?

What percentage of unpurchased content is likely to be removed over the course of a year due to publishers withdrawing titles? What is the procedure for removing those records?

If the library terminates its relationship with the vendor at some point in the future, what provisions does the contract or license allow for the library to retain access to the e-books that it purchased?

PROFILING

Can maximum book costs be set differently for different classification areas? For example, can the maximum cost for chemistry be set at $200 and the maximum for fiction at $40?

Does each aggregator collaborate with the library's major book vendor to make profiling and purchasing as seamless as possible?

TECHNICAL SUPPORT

What customization is available? For instance, can the library's logo be incorporated in the records?

Will the vendor supply high-quality MARC records? Are these included, or is there an additional cost for them? Do the records support ADA access and, if so, how? How are the records supplied, and how often? After a purchase, how does the temporary record change to a permanent one?

How easy is to delete titles, preferably in a batch mode, if the library decided to remove unused books after a certain time interval?

How easy will it be to remove titles from the proposed initial title load that duplicate books the library already owns either in print and as e-books?

How easy is it to suppress titles temporarily, such as over the summer when activity on a college campus may be minimal?

Can the vendor supply a small batch of sample records in advance so that technical services staff can explore and test workflow procedures? Librarians will also want to assess the quality of the records.

TRIGGER EVENT

How much free browsing time is allowed before the user triggers a rental or a purchase?

What circumstances trigger a purchase? How customizable is the trigger?

USABILITY

Analyze the e-book platforms and rate them for features such as being user-friendly, attractive, and/or intuitive.

Can the e-books be downloaded to e-readers or other portable devices? Which ones?

Test functionality such as downloading, printing, and copy/paste. Does the vendor place any restrictions on how much of a single title a patron may print?

If the vendor uses a checkout model, will users be turned away if they try to access titles that are checked out?

VENDOR SERVICES

What standard reports are available? Can custom reports be generated? Is there a staff interface with special reports or statistics? Can the vendor provide samples?

What future enhancements does the vendor plan to offer? When talking with colleagues who are already working with the vendor, ask if any of their ideas for improvement have been implemented.

Does the vendor provide both invoicing and deposit account options? What safeguards are in place to prevent overspending the budget?

Are there any annual fees or hosting fees beyond the costs for buying the books triggered by patron use?

Washington State University developed a useful approach to considering various features and comparing several aggregators.[50]

It would be wise not to focus too much energy on all of the differences between the vendors. Determine which features are the most important for the e-book PDA trial or program. Does one vendor clearly excel at those few features? If all vendors' products and services seem about equal, then focus on the patron experience. Users will not care about the availability of MARC records, the ease of loading weekly updates, or the pricing model; they may care about the ease of using the e-book platform, the amount of material that they can print, or the ability to download books to a portable reading device. Also note that since no single vendor can supply all available e-books, the challenge may be how to blend PDA services from multiple sources rather than selecting one over another.

Developing the E-Book Profile

Although it is possible simply to load the aggregator's e-book list into the OPAC for the trial, most librarians will want to undertake at least some tailoring in the interests of making project funds last as long as possible and of spending them as wisely as possible. Most pilots will last only as long as the allocated funds can support them. Librarians embarking on an e-book PDA pilot should be willing to earmark a significant amount of money to the program; an initial budget of only $10,000, for example, will not last long and the resulting number of purchases may not be enough to yield meaningful assessment results.

Setting up the profile may be a time-consuming task. It may be tempting to consider taking short cuts for the pilot project. For example, librarians might decide that it is easier only to include records for books published during the past two years than to develop a detailed profile. However, if the librarians expect that when the project moves past the pilot stage they will want an e-book record pool covering the past five years, for example, then the purchasing results from the pilot may not give an accurate idea of the kinds of e-books patrons want nor the expected annual cost of the full-fledged program.

Unlike the ILL book programs in which requests are vetted individually by a staff member applying criteria, most e-book PDA requests have no human oversight once the program is implemented. For this reason, it is important to tailor the profile as well as possible. However, also keep in mind that a few "oddball" titles may slip through. Although this is expected and unavoidable, remember that these are books that matched the profile; if they are truly anomalies then it is unlikely that patrons will use them.

Timing

For academic libraries, choose a busy semester rather than a quiet summer.

Maximum Costs and Mediation

What is the maximum cost per book that librarians are willing to spend? Set this amount at a realistic level; setting it too low will result in a much smaller pool of available e-books.

Some e-book aggregators offer an option for patrons to indicate an interest in particular titles that exceed the established cost limit, thus sending an e-mail to a librarian who then makes the purchase decision. However, this process delays the patrons' access to the title, possibly by several days over a weekend, and compromises the transparency of the PDA process. It may be better simply to exclude titles over the price limit and thus avoid this extra layer of complexity. One vendor representative mentioned to the author that librarians almost always approved requests for titles over the maximum cost limit and so wondered how useful this feature really was.

Single- or Multiple-User Access

Some aggregators sell e-books with either a single-user option or a multiple-user option. In general, a multiuser option costs more. Librarians should consider how likely it will be that more than one user will need to access the same content simultaneously. It may be very likely at a public library with a package of popular titles, but far less likely for most books in an academic library. If the librarian expects multiuser access to be relatively rare, choose single-user access to save money, but monitor usage statistics and communication from the vendor to pinpoint those few titles for which upgrades to multiuser access should be purchased. As the ability to download e-books to mobile devices becomes more common, the multiple-user license will become more important since with a single-user license the content of the e-book would be inaccessible for the period of time the title is downloaded to the mobile device. User frustration with checked out e-books is well documented.

Checkout Model

Some vendors allow a short free browsing period of a few minutes. After this interval, users receive a message inviting them to check out the title for a certain period of time, or offering a choice between several time periods, such as one, three, or five days. If the user decides to continue using the book, a rental fee is triggered for the amount of time chosen. Librarians set these intervals when setting up the PDA program. The rental fee itself is set by the publishers and is typically about 10 percent of the purchase price for a twenty-four-hour checkout, although prices can vary significantly.

Purchase Triggers

Different e-book aggregators have different models, and there are usually several levels of each model. There are also different definitions of what constitutes a use, view, browse, or print, often depending on the length of time a user spends with a title; or whether the user browsed the table of contents, index, or text; or how many pages were printed. Librarians can choose immediate purchase as soon as a patron clicks on a book title, but doing this may result in buying many books that users only glanced at. Some activities, such as downloading or printing, immediately trigger a purchase. The rental model is often more attractive, so that the library pays a small fee, often 10 percent of the purchase price, for each of the first X uses and only buys the book after a predetermined number of uses have been reached. This approach ultimately results in some rental payments for books the library never ultimately purchases. It also means that if the purchase is triggered on the fourth use, for example, the library might pay 130 percent of the purchase price: $10 each time patrons used the book for the first three rentals, plus the purchase price on the fourth use. Most e-book aggregators gather information about user trends and can provide information about the most cost effective way to set the purchase triggers. Be sure that the license specifies perpetual access rather than just a subscription to the titles that patrons select.

Publication Date

Decide what date range of publications should be included. Clarify with the vendor if the dates associated with the e-books are truly the publication dates of the equivalent print books. After limiting the e-book PDA trial to imprints within the current three years, librarians at Ohio State University were surprised when analyzing the results to find that patrons had viewed books as old as 1866.[51] Some publishers list the digitization date instead of the actual publication date, which may vary by as much as several decades.

Static or Growing Pool of Records?

After finalizing the profile and removing titles that duplicate library hold-ings, the vendor will announce how many thousands of e-book records will be available to add to the library's OPAC. Librarians then need to decide if, for the pilot, only that initial pool should be used, or whether new titles should be added, probably weekly, as they become available. While a static pool is easier to manage, assimilating new records better emulates full implementation conditions; gives staff a chance to test work-flow procedures; and ultimately gives librarians a better idea how much a fully implemented program will cost. Librarians should review the initial title list before it is loaded; they may notice some obvious factor what was overlooked and needs correcting before loading the titles into the catalog.

Subject

Are there some subjects that would be appropriate to delete from the title offerings? For example, if an academic library does not have a law school, removing all or most legal titles from the list might be appropriate.

Treatment or Level

Most book vendors allow librarians to profile books by treatment or level. Academic librarians might want to exclude textbooks, for instance, or pro-fessional books in all but a few disciplines. Do librarians want to exclude titles in the "For Dummies" or similar series because the treatment is too popular, or include them because they provide helpful overviews to many subjects? Would librarians at a small college want to exclude books with advanced subject treatment, or include them in the catalog to gauge use by faculty and upper level students?

Textbooks

Given the escalating costs of print textbooks, students would welcome elec-tronic editions, especially if there were ways that each student could track his or her own notes and highlighting. The concept of one or two electronic copies available through the library for simultaneous access by multiple users sounds wonderful. Students would be able to avoid the high cost of buying textbooks and the traditional reserves concept of one book at a time for one student for a limited time period during library hours would be a thing of the past. Publishers, however, do not always embrace this model for understandable reasons. Some of them provide electronic textbooks on their own platforms, but at a price that recovers their investment in the new format. Student may be lucky and find that some supplemental readings are available in their libraries as part of e-books plans and collections, but typically not textbooks. Some e-book aggregators offer separate e-reserve options for both chapters and books.

Other Exclusions

If the library has purchased all-inclusive e-book packages with major publishers, titles by these publishers should be excluded from the PDA program. Librarians work with the vendor to exclude all books that the library already owns in e-book format, and should make a decision whether or not to exclude any titles available locally in print. Sending ISBN lists to the vendor is an easy way to accomplish this.

Managing Records for Purchased Books

Technical services staff will be interested in procedures for changing records from temporary ones to permanent records as patron use triggers purchases. This workflow may include sending OCLC the information that the library now owns these e-books.

Relationship of E-book PDA Plan to Approval and Slip Plans

A library book vendor offers tens of thousands of titles. Libraries cannot afford all of them and, in fact, only a relatively small subset will be appropriate purchases for any specific library. Librarians set up a profile with the vendor to tailor the number of books sent on approval (now somewhat of a misnomer since many libraries order shelf-ready books and no longer have the option of returning books they do not want). Other titles that librarians may or may not want to purchase are announced on slips. This term is also now a misnomer; what once arrived in bundles of paper slips is now distributed to selectors via e-mail. Librarians select titles from among the slips and place firm orders for them using the vendor's online database.

How does the e-book PDA profile fit in with approval and slip plans?

Librarians can take one of several approaches. They could decide to continue receiving print approval books, those titles that librarians judge most closely match what the library's patrons need; the slip plan could go on hold for the pilot project and instead those records could be added to the library's OPAC for patrons to select during the normal course of their discovery process. Alternatively, the records for the slip plan books could be added to the OPAC for patrons to find, but librarians could continue to receive and order from slips. To avoid ordering titles twice, it would be important that only one instance of the title appear in the catalog; if a librarian purchases a title in print or as an e-book, the corresponding temporary PDA record should be removed from the catalog. Finally, librarians could decide to load PDA records from a larger universe of available e-books (excluding titles already held, titles from e-book package publishers, or titles in subjects not taught at that university). The records would include many titles that do not match the library's profile, but which might meet its patrons' needs. Part of the evaluation process would involve determining if the out-of-profile titles that patrons purchase through their use of them indeed out-of-scope for the library, or if most of them reflect interdisciplinary or new study areas and are therefore good additions.

Usage Statistics

The e-book aggregator should be able to provide up-to-date, easy-to-understand usage statistics, usually through a website to which selected library staff can obtain access via a log in and password. In addition, the aggregator may also send standard monthly summaries by email. Not only do librarians want to know what titles have been purchased and how much they cost, they also want information about how many times various titles have been accessed. Being able to sort by subject area or call number is also helpful. While patron names are not provided for privacy reasons, it is helpful to be able to tell if usage for particular titles was by one patron or several.

Duration

Unless it has been extremely generously funded, a pilot lasts until the project funds have been exhausted, perhaps only a few months. Ideally, however, librarians should try to fund the pilot for a significant period of time, such as for six months or at least a semester.

Publicity

As with the ILL print purchase program, most libraries will implement their e-book PDA program without fanfare. Patrons may never know that by clicking on an e-book in the OPAC and reading it for some period of time, they triggered a rental or a purchase. In fact, it may be wise to avoid any external publicity about the program to prevent eager patrons from accessing (and thus purchasing) every title in their areas of interest, whether they intend to use them or not.

Records Management

If librarians have so instructed, the e-book aggregator, following the profile instructions, will start adding new titles as they are published. Typically the vendor's database indicates which titles the library has added to its catalog as part of the PDA program to help avoid duplicate purchases. However, librarians also need to keep the vendor informed of the books they buy in print or from other e-book suppliers. When e-books are purchased, the records need to become permanent additions to the OPAC. When funds are exhausted, records for unpurchased books should to be suppressed or removed if the pilot does not move directly into a regular program.

Payment

Librarians can arrange payment on a deposit account basis against which future purchases are charged. These funds can be replenished as needed. Alternatively, the aggregator bills the library at certain intervals until librarians indicate that the pilot funding has been exhausted. The disadvantage of the second option is that billing lags behind activity; by the time the librarians realize that the budget has been exhausted, patrons may have been triggering purchases for several more weeks.

Pilot Assessment

The e-book aggregator provides usage statistics, usually through a web site that program administrators can access. Typically a small evaluation team reviews and assesses the purchases from the pilot project. The team may consist of the primary PDA administrator, as well as designated colleagues from acquisitions, collections, and several subject areas. To investigate, the team will ask many questions. See figure 2.

Considerations for Evaluating an E-book Pilot Project

Do most of the purchased books fall within the scope of the library's collection development policy? If not, is it because a new area of interest now suggests an update to the policy, or because the e-book PDA profile should be adjusted to exclude a less suitable category of books?

What is the distribution of the purchased books by broad subject areas? Do the usage patterns suggest some subject areas that should be "beefed up" in the collection?

If the usage statistics indicate length of time spent in each book, how does length of use correlate with number of uses?

What is the average cost of both rentals and purchases?

Do books in certain subjects receive significantly higher use than others and, if so, do these trends suggest ways to adjust the profile?

How many titles are in the e-book PDA pool? Of those, how many were accessed, but not enough to trigger a purchase? How many triggered a purchase? How many were not used at all?

If the library uses a rental model, what percentage of funds is being spent on browses and what percentage on purchases? Do the results suggest that an adjustment should be made in the number of uses before the purchase trigger?

Feedback

There is no way to solicit patron feedback for an e-book PDA plan in the way that it is possible in a print ILL PDA program. Patrons usually cannot tell the difference between a PDA e-book record in the catalog and a record for an e-book that the library has already purchased. Librarians typically do not want patrons to be able to detect the difference as they access and read the titles they need. Patron feedback is inferred by the patrons' use of certain titles.

When the program moves from the pilot phase into normal operations, there are many more assessment questions to investigate when librarians have more than a few months of data to examine (see Ongoing Assessment).

Funding the Pilot Program and Beyond

The money to fund the pilot program may come from the monograph allocation, special one-time funds, gift money, or other sources. Librarians should remember that, if successful, the e-book PDA will become part of the library's overall collection development strategy, not something "extra" off to the side to fund or not as the budget permits. Schell suggests that "a reasonable starting target for e-book expenditures is 10 percent of a library's total collection budget, working up to 25 percent as users demand it," although remember that e-book acquisitions also occur outside the PDA project.[52] Tenopir reports that one library spend half its monograph budget on patron-driven acquisitions and expects that it may reach 100 percent someday.[53]

E-Book PDA beyond the Pilot Phase

Librarians identify funds to pay for e-book PDA for the whole year, generally extrapolating from the length of the pilot project to determine how much money should be in the PDA fund. Patron-driven acquisitions becomes part of the library's overall collection development plan; rather than being a program beyond traditional collection development, PDA in fact replaces part of the plan and should thus be allocated part of the overall funding. The funding can come from various subject areas proportionate to the percentage of books patrons selected in those subjects during the pilot phase. For example, if 15 percent of the purchased books fell into the engineering subject area, perhaps about 15 percent of the e-book PDA fund should come from the engineering monograph budget. Another approach is to take the e-book PDA funds "off the top" and then allocate the remainder to the various traditional collection development funds in the usual manner. Librarians still have a role in selecting some materials for the library, but patrons' needs and uses now drive part of it.

After evaluating the pilot program, librarians may alter the PDA profile in some way, perhaps changing the per-book maximum cost, adding or deleting subject areas, or tweaking other areas, such as adding or dropping fiction. Periodic evaluation of recently selected books as well as ongoing usage analysis of purchased titles will suggest other changes over time. If librarians notice heavy purchasing patterns among several publishers' titles, for example, it may be time to explore purchasing those publishers' entire or subject e-book packages at a greater savings than buying e-books one at a time through an aggregator. If this is done, remember to exclude those publishers from the PDA profile.

How long should untouched PDA titles sit in a library's catalog before being removed? Since e-book PDA programs are in their infancy, there is no consensus yet based on practice or experience. Some purchased library books often sit untouched for years on library shelves; why should a PDA plan be different? The OPACs at many academic libraries include many records linked to older full text items, such as to HathiTrust titles; many of these titles may never be used at a particular library, but they are readily accessible should someone need them. Can the same argument be made for PDA titles? There is currently no cost to the library to keep the records in the OPAC, so why not leave them there? Are there any major drawbacks to the record for a 2012 e-book sitting in the OPAC until 2015 or 2025 before someone first views it? The librarians have simply provided a larger pool of items from which their patrons can draw; the length of time that the records stay in the OPAC should not matter. The main issue is that as time goes on, the pool of books grows larger and thus the potential number of books that might be purchased after user interactions grows (along with the cost) as patrons occasionally choose older titles. Librarians may want to monitor certain types of books periodically, such as computer programming titles, to remove any selected unpurchased ones that have reached the end of their useful lives. But some books in areas such as literary criticism or history may not see their first use until several years after being added to the catalog. However, if librarians decide to remove some or all of the unpurchased titles after a certain time interval, the vendor will recommend ways to remove them in a batch.

Relationship to ILL

How does e-book PDA affect interlibrary loan operations? It does so in two major ways. ILL staff typically first search systems like OCLC's WorldCat and, in the absence of any indication of local holdings, order items from other libraries. This procedure is efficient and effective because the majority of ILL requests are not held locally. In the new model, the library has just added potentially tens of thousands of e-book records to the OPAC that may *not* be reflected in WorldCat because the library has not bought them yet and may in fact never buy the majority of them. However, it makes little sense for the ILL staff to buy a book in print or to incur costs by borrowing it from another library if the e-book version is a mouse-click away in the OPAC. Collections librarians and ILL librarians should begin conversations about how to coordinate these two functions so that library staff connect patrons to the books they need in the most cost-effective manner and in the format that the patron prefers. Some librarians have reported successful solutions involving collaborations between interlibrary loan and collections and/or acquisitions.[54] ILL librarians managing print purchase programs may want to talk with their collections and/or acquisitions colleagues to explore expanding the ILL plan so that, if available, e-books will be purchased for patrons instead of print. Even if some e-books need a day or two to be activated from a vendor other than the e-book PDA aggregator, the patron will in most cases get access to the material faster than physical delivery of a print book through the mail. As an added bonus, the title becomes part of the permanent collection for others to use in the future.

At least one aggregator avoids the OCLC conundrum described above by arranging for its customers' e-book PDA records to come *from* OCLC both for the initial load and for subsequent updates. Then not only are the records of high quality, but the library's PDA e-book holdings are also reflected in WorldCat. With this arrangement, be sure that the license with the PDA aggregator allows providing book chapters through interlibrary lending, since other libraries may occasionally place requests for them.

It seems reasonable to suppose that if librarians add several tens of thousands of e-book records to their OPACs, at least some of these e-books will meet patron needs that previously were fulfilled with interlibrary loan requests. Over time, it is possible that the number of requests for ILL loans may decline as a result, resulting in some cost savings for ILL. If this happens, however, it may be difficult to establish a direct correlation between improved access to e-books and declining ILL loan requests. Many patrons do not know about interlibrary loan or, if they do, feel that waiting a week to receive a book loan is too long to meet their needs and thus do not place requests for everything that they might have wanted. ILL book loan requests may decline for other reasons, too, such as the increasing incidence of full text older material (pre-1923) in Google Books and government documents in HathiTrust. Or ILL loan requests may continue to increase as has generally been the case in many academic libraries; any decline because of increased local access to e-books may be offset by increases for other reasons.

Ongoing Assessment

For the first few years of normal operations, a librarian or evaluation team continues to monitor and assess the program fairly frequently. Many of the same evaluation points that were relevant during the pilot project assessment continue to be important and are repeated here. There are also some additional points that can better be assessed after the number of purchased titles reaches a critical mass. See figure 3.

Unlike in the ILL book purchase program, patron information is generally unavailable because of privacy concerns and because of IP range authentication rather than individual log on. However, it should be possible to determine if titles are used by one or by multiple users.

There will always be some books that do not receive much use past the initial purchase, but if the profile is sound, these should be a relatively low percentage of the total. Overall, and over time, patron-selected e-book purchases should more or less follow the same pattern as print books acquired through ILL purchase plans: in general, they should receive higher use than similar librarian-selected books.

Time will tell if these assumptions are correct. It is possible that results for e-book PDA purchases and subsequent use may be at least partially skewed by patrons' ability to "dabble" by opening and closing a lot of e-books in their search for the work that best meets their needs. Still, the purchased e-books met the librarian-crafted profile and most should thus provide solid value.

Since e-book PDA programs are still fairly new as of this writing, published examples of their evaluation are scarce. Hodges and her colleagues report the results of the e-book PDA pilot at Ohio State University.[55] Price and McDonald's study covered four years of e-book PDA at the Claremont Colleges.[56] Be aware that the evaluations of early programs may not reflect PDA plan refinements and options that are now available.

Postpurchase Management

One of the virtues of e-books is that they take no shelf space. They do not need to shelved or shifted. E-books do not even take up any local server space since the OPAC links to the provider's server. It may be tempting to buy e-books and then forget about them. Many libraries' e-book collections are so new that there is currently little reason to worry about managing them after purchase. However, almost all library collections, even in academic research libraries, require periodic assessment and post-purchase management. In the print world, academic librarians deselect or weed collections periodically, often moving less-used material to off-site storage facilities, deselecting additional copies of older material, and withdrawing older editions. Public librarians purchase far less often using the just-in-case model and also weed more often so that their collections reflect the current interests of their customers.

As their e-book collections grow, whether from their own selection efforts or through those of their patrons, librarians should consider and plan occasional assessment activity. Should older editions be removed? Should titles with no or low usage be suppressed and, if so, after what time interval? Academic librarians usually do not consider removing print books until several decades have passed with no- or low-use; is the weeding threshold similar for e-books?

5) Alternatives to PDA

PRINT BOOKS THROUGH THE OPAC

Librarians at a number of academic libraries have experimented with patron-driven
acquisitions models for print books through
the OPAC. In this model, librarians profile
print-only titles from their book vendor's
catalog, very much as described earlier for
the e-book model. MARC records for these
titles are added to the OPAC with a special
embedded note in one field, such as the 856
field, to trigger a special note in the record
display. When patrons encounter these titles,
the note invites them to log in to place an
order, often with options to indicate desired
delivery speed.

In this model patrons must be given
some explanation about why the title is in the
catalog but is not immediately available. The
explanation should be short, but clearly indicate that the library will be buying the book
(the patron will not be charged) and provide
good information about the average number

of business days that it will take before the book is available for each of several delivery options.

Librarians have used this model successfully both with profiles covering most subject areas and with profiles for only a few subject areas. Librarians at one institution experimented with loading records for selected publishers from which they had previously purchased the entire annual output in print. They discovered that users generated orders for only a small fraction of that output, saving the library thousands of dollars and focusing on acquiring only those titles that patrons actually used. At another library, most of the titles formerly included in the approval plan were moved into this print PDA model; the patrons, rather than the librarians, decided which books would be added to the collection. In another case, libraries in a consortium with a shared catalog experimented with this model.

Vendor

Librarians can let orders flow seamlessly from the ordering point to the supplying vendor, typically the book jobber whose inventory file provided the titles selected for the catalog. Alternatively, the orders can be routed to Acquisitions so staff can choose the fastest supplier among a range of potential vendors. When the books arrive and are cataloged, staff change or update the temporary catalog record to a permanent one.

Relationship with E-books

This model can be tricky to manage because of the varying speed with which publishers issue e-books after the print books are released. If librarians prefer e-books over print, then consider setting up a short term embargo, perhaps ninety days, after the publication is in print before loading titles into the catalog. If the e-book has not been issued by the end of the embargo period, then the record for the print book can be loaded; however, if the e-book is available, then the e-book record would be preferred. The goal would be to avoid having records for the same unpurchased titles in both print and electronic versions since librarians would generally not wish patrons to trigger purchases in both formats. However, some librarians are experimenting with offering both print and electronic versions when available, and giving patrons the choice of ordering the format they prefer. This model can be used alone, or in conjunction with an e-book PDA plan (see Hybrid PDA Models below).

Assessment

Assessment would be similar to that for other PDA models. If the library offers patrons a choice of print and electronic, when available, it would be particularly useful to know if patrons display a significant preference for one format over another and, if so, whether this preference varies by subject or over time. Subsequent use is also important to track.

Records Management

As with the e-book PDA model, at some point librarians decide to remove the records for unpurchased print books from the catalog. In the past this step might have taken place fairly fast since many books go out of print quickly, but with the advent of print on demand (see below) this consideration is now less of a concern. Many books published within the past few years can now be printed as single copies and delivered almost as quickly as titles in vendors' warehouses.

Information Technology Support

Implementing this model often requires support from the library's information technology department to develop the OPAC messages, to route the requests to the acquisitions department or directly to the book vendor, and to automate other ordering processing steps.

HYBRID PDA MODEL: PRINT AND ELECTRONIC

Librarians who already have a print PDA plan, whether an ILL purchase on demand programs for print books and DVDs or the print PDA plan with OPAC records supplied from a book vendor, may be interested in branching out to include e-book PDA plans. Librarians at institutions that have not had a print PDA plan may wish to begin their venture in PDA with an integrated plan for material in both formats.

Efforts to coordinate both formats may involve close collaboration between two areas that often do not share reporting lines: interlibrary loan and acquisitions/collections. With the primary objective of filling patrons' requests quickly, efficiently, and cost-effectively, librarians work to develop seamless, comprehensive, and easy-to-manage workflows. It is especially important to coordinate the plans so that the same titles are not inadvertently purchased in multiple formats unless there is a particular reason to do so in specific cases. As mentioned previously, it is also important that ILL develop a workflow to include checking patrons' new loan requests to see if there are unpurchased e-book records for them in the catalog. Alerting patrons to e-books a click or two away is faster than buying or borrowing the print book. It may not always be less expensive than borrowing the print book, but e-books in the OPAC as part of the PDA plan are ones that match the profile and that should have a greater likelihood of subsequent use—exactly the kind of book that librarians want to make available in the local collection.

One library that met this challenge in an innovative way is SUNY-Geneseo. Librarians integrated new software, the Getting It System Toolkit (GIST) with ILLiad, an interlibrary loan management system. GIST provides tools and workflows that combine interlibrary loan and just-in-time acquisitions services and supports purchase request processing and cooperative collection development efforts by providing rich information that informs the borrow/buy decision. GIST provides users and library staff with data, such as uniqueness of the requested item, free online sources, reviews and rankings, and purchasing options and prices. The software lets patrons indicate preferred format and whether they want a loan or a purchase. Library staff make the final determination based on factors like availability and price, but the workflow depends on being able to pass the requests quickly and easily between interlibrary loan and acquisitions, while keeping patrons in the loop with status updates.[57] GIST (http://idsproject.org/tools/gist.aspx) is freely available but does require ILLiad as a platform.

The Texas A & M Libraries funds Suggest a Purchase for patrons to place requests for material they need. Over a three-year period, librarians bought 9,825 items for users in a variety of formats; subsequent analysis showed that most of them were appropriate for an academic library.[58]

INNOVATIVE SERVICES

Most librarians will probably establish their PDA programs along one or both of two general lines: based on interlibrary loan requests that meet certain criteria, or based on patron use or requests from OPAC records of unpurchased titles in either print or electronic formats.

However, there is room for innovative approaches. For instance, Barnhart describes course-integrated collection development in which students enrolled in a research methods class followed guidelines to select library materials in support of their coursework.[59] Squires and Laurence worked with schoolchildren in a project "to give children a chance to input into our stock selection, and to improve our own knowledge and understanding of children's reading needs and preferences."[60]

Scan-on-Demand

Many libraries support in-house digitization projects, often of special collections material or other local or institutional collections and papers. While most have a collections-driven plan to prioritize the material they wish to digitize, many have also made provisions for scanning items out of sequence in response to patron requests. The request may take a few days to complete and there may be a charge for the service, especially for users who are not affiliated with the library. Besides filling a single user's need, the item or its bibliographic information is often added to the library's site so that others can view or order it. The Boston Public Library scans books to fill out-of-copyright ILL lending requests and posts them to the Internet Archive's Open Content Alliance. Not only does the original requestor gain access to the work within a day, but the title is also available to future users.[61]

Print-on-Demand

With print on demand (POD), also sometimes called publish on demand, book copies are printed and distributed only when orders for them have been placed. The development of digital printing has made this service economically feasible. Once mainly serving self-publishing authors, these services now contract with small publishers with specialty titles, or even with larger ones that want to be able to provide single copies from their backlists on demand. Several book wholesalers have print-on-demand divisions that serve the library and bookstore markets. A few university libraries offer certain out-of-print and out-of-copyright titles on a POD basis for a fee, either through a distributor or on their own.

POD has sometimes been referred to as long tail publishing. While there is not much profit in providing any single copy, the cumulative effect of providing many special-interest or out-of-print books can be profitable.[62]

The next step in print-on-demand service centers on selling libraries the machines that produce print-on-demand books. Prompted by patron requests for books that are not available locally, staff can search the vendor's list of available titles and, if the needed titles are there, let the machine print and bind them. To recover the relatively high costs of both the machine and the book content, most libraries with such a machine sell these books to patrons. The major advantage is that this process eliminates the time and cost needed to deliver a physical book from another library, publisher, bookstore, or wholesaler. In addition, there are often customization options, such as printing in a large font for users with vision impairments. At a conference, the author heard speakers from one enterprising library mention brisk sales of blank books using a selection of cover art reproduced from items in the special collections department.

The options for any of these models are to focus on titles in the public domain for which royalties do not need to be paid; to focus on more recent, low- or short-demand titles for which royalties are due; or to combine the two. Some vendors have now moved beyond seeing their customers as self-publishing authors and book wholesalers; they now reach out directly to consumers via internet platforms. These vendors may combine both electronic and print book models; users might be able to read titles online at no cost, but must pay to have them printed. An executive at one company says that the goal "is to enable any book ever published to be available to anyone, whenever they want it, in its original edition or one customized by the buyer."[63]

⑥ Cons

This book examines the many positive aspects of adopting patron-driven acquisitions programs. There are some potentially negative aspects, however.

RESOURCE SHARING

Sharing e-books is often difficult or impossible. Licensing agreements sometimes prohibit providing chapters from e-books, although the astute electronic resources librarian will try to amend resource sharing restrictions when negotiating the licenses. Even when a licensing agreement does allow providing chapters, it may be difficult for the local interlibrary loan staff to determine quickly and easily which e-books out of thousands permit this activity. In addition, ILL staff at the borrowing institutions may not even bother to request a chapter from an e-book based on previous experience.

There is also no practical way to lend an entire e-book, which is why some librarians decide not to pursue e-book PDA plans.[64] At a conference, the author heard an interesting suggestion that publishers consider offering direct short-term access to their e-book titles by essentially charging a rental fee. Librarians, patrons, or independent scholars might well be willing to pay a reasonable credit card charge for short-term access to books, thus creating an alternative revenue stream for publishers while meeting researchers' immediate needs at a reasonable price. Journal publishers already do this for articles, although in many cases the publishers' notion of a reasonable price does not always coincide with that of the potential user.

COSTS

Some librarians seem less inclined to consider PDA programs in times of tight budgets. There is no extra money, they declare, to set aside for patron selections. This reasoning should be examined carefully. In difficult economic times, surely it is even more important that scarce collection development resources be spent on material with a higher-than-average likelihood of being used? Studies have shown that patron-selected print books have a significantly higher subsequent use pattern.[65] A PDA-purchased book has a guarantee of at least one use, whereas a librarian-selected book has, on average, a much lower chance of being used.

Finding the money to fund a PDA pilot project can prove a challenge, since a reasonably large sum is advisable to give the plan a chance of remaining viable for as long as six or twelve months so that there will be sufficient data to analyze. Collection managers may have access to one-time funds, or may take a percentage off the top of the monograph budget, or may earmark parts of allocated funds for the project. Selectors may understandably prefer that their budgets remain intact until the results of the pilot demonstrate the value of the PDA approach.

There is the fear that an e-book PDA program could run through a budget quickly. Very early PDA experiments ran this risk, but current and evolving models offer better balance between a few rented uses in relation to a purchase based in significant use. Librarians can also monitor these programs almost in real time, and the vendors can impose expenditure caps that prevent new purchases once the maximum has been reached. Vendors can usually also suggest ways to tailor a profile to match the budget, based on their experience with similar customers. One library limited purchases to one per patron per day; another required staff mediation for purchases more than fifty dollars.[66] While this author does not advocate such limitations, it is possible to impose them.

Another concern revolves around the twin concepts of paying rental fees for some books that the library never actually buys, coupled with the fact that when patron use triggers a purchase after a certain number of uses, the library has by then paid considerably more than list price for the book. The trade-off is that thousands of e-book titles are available for instant use by the library's patrons; users choose the ones that best meet their needs. Many titles are never used and thus incur no direct costs. Paying a rental fee of 10 or 20 percent of the list price for each use is generally far less expensive in terms of both direct and indirect costs than obtaining the books through interlibrary loan. The actual purchases cost more, but these are books that patrons have selected as meeting their information needs; the expectation is that these patron-selected books will see greater use in the future.

STAFF TIME

The time needed to work with vendors (often both the e-book aggregator and also the book vendor) is significant. Developing the profile, or even editing an existing approval plan profile, is time consuming. Analyzing the pilot project data and reporting it to administrators and colleagues are also time-intensive. Ongoing assessment represents another time commitment, as does working to coordinate and analyze print and e-book PDA plans, if both are being used. Ongoing maintenance is also a commitment, as records flow in and out frequently. Besides the initial record load and the periodic arrival of new titles, work is also needed to overlay prior records with newer ones, and to remove some titles due to publisher withdrawals or the arrival of newer editions.

Not all records are as complete or robust as librarians would prefer. At the author's institution, many initial records came with the single subject heading Electronic Books. These were later replaced with better records.

Assistance from the local information technology staff is often needed to implement and support the PDA plan. For libraries that combine their print and electronic holdings of a title in one record, IT assistance may be needed to add the links to the e-books for titles already held in print, if librarians did not elect to deduplicate, or if librarians implement a hybrid

PDA plan with instances of both print and electronic versions of books for patrons to choose between. Some of the functions of implementing and maintaining the PDA program can be automated, but usually only with IT assistance.

EFFECTS ON THE COLLECTION

Some librarians worry that implementing a PDA program will skew the collection in undesirable ways. Perhaps a few patrons will each trigger dozens of purchases, all in concentrated subject areas. The author found that the vast majority of patrons only received a few purchased books each as a result of normal ILL requesting activity, perhaps because many patrons only request a few titles in the course of their academic work. For example, after the first thirty months of the Purdue's ILL book purchase program, 1,943 books had been bought for 810 different patrons; more than half of the users only received one book each and the average was 2.4 books each.[67] It was certainly true that a handful of heavy ILL users received many purchased books, but these met the purchase criteria and joined the pool of others that received higher than average subsequent circulation. A professor with an active research interest in a very obscure research area will in general not skew the permanent collection through ILL PDA because many of the requested titles will not meet the selection criteria; some will be too old or too expensive, in a foreign language, or so specialized that an online bookseller does not stock them for immediate shipment. Interlibrary loan will fill those requests. Houle found that in a two-year period 1.8 books were purchased per ILL user.[68] In the e-book model or in the model of records for print books added to the catalog, the pool of titles available for purchase based on patron use or request has been created based on a librarian-created profile. Hussong-Christian and Goergen-Doll make the important point that in most cases the patrons themselves have exercised their judgment and criteria to determine that certain books that the local library does not own are important enough to them to place an interlibrary loan request. Combined with the library's selection criteria, there are thus actually two filters in place to assure that the library buys relevant titles with a high likelihood of subsequent use; in fact, the library may actually be leveraging its patrons' expertise in emerging and cutting edge research areas to assist with collection development.[69]

There is a fear that despite all safeguards, some inappropriate material will end up in the collection. While it is true that at least some marginal or borderline material may be purchased, the instances should be very low if the criteria or profiles are well-crafted and well-applied. Remember that in traditional collection development plenty of material that will never be used is also added to the collection. PDA plans are not completely risk free from acquiring a few questionable titles, but the incidence should be very low.

Ingold raises the interesting point that at least some users may go straight to interlibrary loan rather than reviewing locally available material that might meet their needs. She wonders if ILL often borrows or buys books for patrons on topics that are perfectly well covered by the titles already in the local collection.[70] This situation may be true, but it is also true that patron-selected titles subsequently circulate far more frequently, on average, than the titles already in the collection. There must be something about them that appeals not only to the initial requestor but also to subsequent users that is absent from similar titles. There is usually a strong correlation between usage and what patrons consider relevant to their research and learning needs, however hard that may be to define.

One current downside of e-book PDA is that not all publishers have yet hopped on the e-book bandwagon or, if they have, some engage in unhelpful practices such as releasing e-book editions months after the print versions or declining to make titles available through aggregators.[71] Some subject areas are well-represented by e-books, but others are not. Pricing between the two formats may be similar or wildly different.

Another concern is that academic librarians have traditionally built collections not only to meet immediate patron needs, but also to meet the long-term and in-depth needs of future scholars. In general, patron-driven acquisitions focuses on acquiring relatively recent material to meet immediate needs. Certainly much of that material will also meet patrons' future needs, but by embracing PDA are librarians turning their backs on longer-term collection development? This is a thorny issue. Some librarians argue that use is not everything, that there are certain titles that particular libraries ought to have because of the importance of the topic, the author, or the publisher. Others might point out that the worthiest titles may not be worth acquiring if patrons never use them or do not express a need for them until years after the acquisition date. There is no way to tell in advance which titles will be the shelf-sitters. Fortunately we live in a time when it is far easier to acquire an out-of-print book than in the past: we can easily identify copies on the used book market; we can often buy an e-book version years after publication; chances are improving all the time that older titles can be printed on demand; interlibrary loan is almost always an option. Some librarians are testing the legal waters by digitizing selected orphan works—titles within the years of copyright protection but for which it appears impossible to identify or locate the rights holder.

Some librarians wonder if similar or peer libraries will wind up with cookie-cutter collections if they all participate in the same e-book PDA plans. This concern may have been more common when the number of players was small and their book lists were new and fairly small. This is not the case today; the e-book aggregators often have well over 200,000 titles in their lists, and these grow daily as they add new publishers, as new titles are published, and as backlists increase. There should soon be no greater danger of similarity between collections than there was when librarians made most of the selection choices and dozens if not hundreds of peer libraries all held a core of very similar titles. The danger of similarity may even be significantly less now that it is the patrons who choose the titles through PDA plans.

Some librarians view patron-driven acquisitions as a way to augment the traditional librarian collection development model when in fact PDA is on track to *replace* part of it. Reluctance to embrace patron-driven acquisitions as more than a marginal experiment may rest in part in the librarians' reluctance to relinquish a cherished role. One of a library's fundamental activities is acquiring material for its user population. Despite the fact that significant numbers of librarian-selected books sit unused for years, many academic librarians seem reluctant to acknowledge that their users might in many cases know better what books are of value, at least in the short- to medium-term. Some of this denial and angst may be rooted in the current environment of rapid workplace change. Perhaps librarians are less concerned about letting patrons choose books than they are about their own changing roles. The need to cling to familiar tasks manifests itself in an unenthusiastic response to new models for new times.[72]

7 Future Directions

The worlds of scholarship, publishing, and libraries are changing faster than ever. Less information passes through the long publishing process; some authors bypass the editorial process altogether by posting directly to the internet or listing their works with online booksellers. Even some large commercial publishers and university presses no longer maintain dozens or hundreds of warehoused copies of their print backlists, but arrange for print-on-demand services through a third party as orders come in. Some libraries have also experimented with local print-on-demand machines.

Another trend is digitization-on-demand. If copyright laws permit digitization and distribution of material that a user needs, then that format is often preferred. Interlibrary loan services have offered this service for years, but best practices designed to address copyright concerns usually limit a user's access to scanned chapters and articles to a few weeks so that libraries are clearly not archiving this material; ILL management software automatically deletes files after a designated period of time. Depending on an item's copyright date and ownership, archives, special collections, and digitization offices can also scan selected titles on demand, sometimes uploading them to local digital collections or institutional repositories on the grounds that a title requested by one user may be of interest to others in the future. These on-demand services can be expensive, especially for lengthy documents; questions soon arise about funding them or offering them on a cost-recovery basis.

Users increasingly prefer mobile devices for reading a wide variety of material; librarians will not only have to be sure that they buy content that their users can download to these devices, but will also need to be familiar with how the burgeoning number of makes, models, and versions access that content. Librarians face the challenge of balancing the needs of tech-savvy users with those of other patrons who prefer print in all or some instances. How much content can a library afford to duplicate in multiple formats?

Will we ever reach a point where library collections are built exclusively or even largely by the people who use them, or will librarians always have a role in guiding collection development? The outcome of Michael Levine-Clark's experiment at the University of Denver is eagerly anticipated; he plans to let patrons select most titles for a year and then compare the purchases against the list of title that the librarians would have ordered, but did not for the experimental year.[73] But even if libraries move more towards patron-driven acquisitions for a larger percentage of their collections, librarians' expertise is still critical for crafting the profiles of books or other materials available for patrons to choose, so that academic librarians do not find that they have a growing collection of pop self-help books and mystery novels or public librarians discover a group of expensive specialized scientific handbooks.

These developments suggest that the roles of the collection development librarian, selector, bibliographer, and subject specialist are changing along with other library roles. While at least some of the material selection will devolve upon the user, the subject specialist and collection manager still play a vital, although changing, role in the organization.[74]

Departmental lines are blurring and shifting as many librarians focus more on the process of filling patrons' requests for materials and less on the distinction between buying or borrowing them. At some libraries, the inter-library loan function has moved into the acquisitions department entirely, while at others the connection between two units that historically had very little interaction has been strengthened.[75]

Looking even farther into the future, it is possible that journal titles may become less important over time as individual journal articles become more important. One can envision a world where patrons choose the articles that they need from a preselected group of journal titles, publishers, or subjects; librarians then buy those individual articles and add them to permanent digital collections, like current e-book PDA programs.

As librarians identify, embrace, and resolve these future opportunities in collection development based on user need, the author encourages librarians exploring innovative solutions to contribute their experiences to the literature. Interesting as it already is, the published record on patron-driven acquisitions in all its aspects probably represents only the tip of the iceberg. How many other interesting experiments and practices flourish in our libraries but are unknown because the innovators have not taken the time to write about them? Let your current colleagues benefit from your experience, and offer future colleagues a glimpse into this exciting moment of evolving user services.

The increasingly rapid and diverse availability of digital material makes the development of patron-driven acquisitions models even more timely and attractive than was possible with print-only models. Librarians can tailor plans to offer their patrons a wider variety of material than ever before, but can limit purchases to those items that users actually need. This model promises an exciting new era in collection development.

selected bibliography

Aguilar, William. 1986. "The Application of Relative Use and Interlibrary Demand in Collection Development." *Collection Management* 8(1): 15–24.

Alder, Nancy Lichten. 2007. "Direct Purchasing as a Function of Interlibrary Loan: Buying Books Versus Borrowing." *Journal of Interlibrary Loan, Document Delivery & Electronic Reserve* 18(1): 9–15.

Allen, G. G. 1988. "The Economic Efficiencies of Alternatives to Purchase and Loan of Library Resources." *IATUL Quarterly* 2(4): 209–14.

Allen, Megan, Suzanne M. Ward, Tanner Wray, and Karl E. Debus-López. 2003. "Patron-focused Services: Cooperative Interlibrary Loan, Collection Development and Acquisitions." *Interlending & Document Supply* 30(2): 138–41.

Anderson, Chris. 2006. *The Long Tail: Why the Future of Business Is Selling Less of More.* New York: Hyperion.

Anderson, Kristine J., Robert S. Freeman, Jean-Pierre V. M. Hérubel, Lawrence J. Mykytiuk, Judith M. Nixon, and Suzanne M. Ward. 2002. "Buy, Don't Borrow: Bibliographers' Analysis of Academic Library Collection Development through Interlibrary Loan Requests." *Collection Management* 27(3/4): 1–11.

———. 2010. "Liberal Arts Books on Demand: A Decade of Patron-driven Collection Development, Part 1." *Collection Management* 35(3/4): 125–41.

Anson, Catherine and Ruth R. Connell. 2009. *E-Book Collections.* Washington, D.C.: Association of Research Libraries.

Badics, Joe. 2004 "Acquisitions and Interlibrary Loan Together: Good Marriage or Will George W. Bush Object?" *Against the Grain* 16(4): 52, 54.

Barnhart, Anne C. 2010. "Want Buy-in? Let Your Students Do the Buying! A Case Study of Course-Integrated Collection Development." *Collection Management* 35(3/4): 237–43.

Bartolo, Laura M. 1989. "Automated ILL Analysis and Collection Development: A Hi-Tech Marriage of Convenience." *Library Acquisitions: Practice and Theory* 13(4): 361–69.

Beaton, Barbara and Jay H. Kirk. 1988. "Application of an Automated Interlibrary Loan Log." *Journal of Academic Librarianship* 14(1): 24–27.

Blake, Julie C., and Susan P. Schleper. 2005. "From Data to Decisions: Using Surveys and Statistics to Make Collection Management Decisions." *Library Collections, Acquisitions, and Technical Services* 28(4): 460–64.

Blummer, Barbara. 2005. "Opportunities for Libraries with Print-on-demand Publishing." *Journal of Access Services* 3(2): 41–54.

Bombeld, Madeleine and Arlene Hanerfeld. 2004. "The Surprising Truth about Faculty Perception and Use of Collection Development Opportunities: One Library's Case Study." *Against the Grain* 16(2): 18, 20, 22.

Bracke, Marianne Stowell. 2010. "Science and Technology Books on Demand: A Decade of Patron-driven Collection Development, Part 2." *Collection Management* 35(3/4): 142–50.

———, Jean-Pierre V. M. Hérubel, and Suzanne M.Ward. 2010. "Some Thoughts on Opportunities for Collection Development Librarians." *Collection Management* 35(3/4): 255–59.

Broadus, Robert N. 1980. "Use Studies of Library Collections." *Library Resources & Technical Services* 24(4): 317–24.

Brug, Sandy and Cristi MacWaters. 2004. "Patron-driven Purchasing from Interlibrary Loan Requests." *Colorado Libraries* 30(3): 36–38.

Byrd, Gary D., D. A. Thomas, and Katherine E. Hughes. 1982. "Collection Development Using Interlibrary Loan Borrowing and Acquisitions Statistics." *Bulletin of the Medical Library Association* 70(1): 1–9.

Campbell, Sharon A. 2006. "To Buy or to Borrow, That Is the Question." *Journal of Interlibrary Loan, Document Supply and Electronic Reserve* 16(3):35–39.

Carrigan, Dennis P. 1996. "Data-guided Collection Development: A Promise Unfulfilled." *College & Research Libraries* 57(5): 429–37.

Carroll, Diane. 2010. "Ebooks: Taking the Next Step." https://research.wsulibs.wsu.edu:8443/jspui/bitstream/2376/2568/1/EBooks%20Taking%20the%20next%20step%20Timberline%20May%202010.pdf (accessed April 23, 2012).

Chan, Gayle Rosemary Y. C. 2004. "Purchase Instead of Borrow: An International Perspective." *Journal of Interlibrary Loan Document Delivery and Information Supply* 14(4): 23–37.

Clendenning, Lynda Fuller. 2001. "Purchase Express for Any User Request: The University of Virginia Library Offers Delivery in Seven Days." *College & Research Libraries News* 62(1): 16–17.

Colford, Michael R. 2008. "Rethinking Resource Sharing: Boston Public Library provides Scan-on-demand for Interlibrary Loan." *Interface* 30(1): 5–6.

Comer, Alberta and Elizabeth A. Lorenzen. 2005. "Biz of Acq: Is Purchase-on-demand a Worthy Model? Do Patrons Really Know What They Want?" *Against the Grain* 17(1): 75–78.

Coopey, Barbara M. and Ann M. Snowman. 2006. "ATG special report: ILL Purchase Express." *Against the Grain* 18(1): 46–49.

Dougherty, William C. 2009. "Print on Demand: What Librarians Should Know." *Journal of Academic Librarianship* 35(2): 184–86.

Foss, Michelle. 2007. "Books-on-demand Pilot Program: An Innovative 'Patroncentric' Approach to Enhance the Library Collection." *Journal of Access Services* 5(1/2): 306–15.

Fountain, Kathleen Carlisle and Linda Frederiksen. 2010. "Just Passing through: Patron-initiated Collection Development in Northwest Academic Libraries." *Collection Management* 35(3/4): 185–95.

Hardesty, Larry. 1981. "Use of Library Materials at a Small Liberal Arts College." *Library Research* 3(3): 261–82.

Herslow-Fex, Anna. 1989. "Interlibrary Loan Statistics: an Instrument for Collection Development." *LIBER Bulletin* 34: 73–75.

Henderson, Albert. 2000. "The Library Collection Failure Quotient: The Ratio of Interlibrary Borrowing to Collection Size." *Journal of Academic Librarianship* 26(3): 159–70.

Hodges, Dracine, Cyndi Preston, and Hamilton, Marsha J. 2010. "Patron-initiated Collection Development: Progress of a Paradigm Shift." *Collection Management* 35(3/4): 208–21.

———. 2010. "Resolving the Challenge of E-Books. *Collection Management* 35(3/4): 196–200.

Houle, Louis. 2004. "Convergence between Interlibrary Loan and Acquisitions: A Science and Engineering Library Experience." *IATUL Proceedings* new series 14: 1–7.

Hulsey, Richard. 2003. "Purchase on Demand: A Better Customer Service Model." *Library Journal* 128(10): 77.

Hussong-Christian, Uta and Kerri Goergen-Doll. 2010. "We're Listening: Using Patron Feedback to Assess and Enhance Purchase on Demand." *Journal of Interlibrary Loan, Document Delivery & Electronic Reserve* 20(5): 319–35.

Ingold, Jane L. 2004. "Buyer Beware: Using Interlibrary Loan Requests in Purchasing Decisions." *Against the Grain* 16(2): 30, 32, 34.

Jackson, Mary E. 1989. "Library to Library." *Wilson Library Bulletin* 64(4): 88–89.

———. 1998. *Measuring the Performance of Interlibrary Loan Operations in North American Research & College Libraries.* Washington, D.C.: Association of Research Libraries.

Kane, Laura Townsend. 1997. "Access vs. Ownership: Do We Have to Make a Choice?" *College & Research Libraries* 58(1): 59–67.

Khalil, Mounir A. 1993. "Applications of an Automated ILL Statistical Analysis as a Collection Development Tool." *Journal of Interlibrary Loan, Document Delivery & Information Supply* 4(1): 45–54.

Kent, Allen. 1979. *Use of Library Materials: The University of Pittsburgh Study.* New York: M. Dekker.

Knievel, Jennifer E., Heather Wicht, and Lynn Silipigni Connaway. 2006. "Use of Circulation Statistics and Interlibrary Loan Data in Collection Management." *College & Research Libraries* 67(1): 35.

Kyrillidou, Martha and Les Bland, eds. 2009. *ARL Statistics 2007–2008.* Washington, D.C.: Association of Research Libraries.

Lahmon, Jo Ann. 1991. "Using Interlibrary Loan Data in Collection Development." *OCLC Micro* 7(5): 19–22.

Levine-Clark, Michael. 2010. "Developing a Multiformat Demand-driven Acquisition Model." *Collection Management* 35(3/4): 201–207.

Livingston, Camille and Antje Mays. 2004. "Using Interlibrary Loan Data as a Selection Tool: ILL Trails Provide Collection Clues." *Against the Grain* 16(2): 22–28.

Lockett, Barbara (ed). 1989. *Guide to the Evaluation of Library Collections.* Chicago: American Library Association.

Mackey, Terry. 1989. "Interlibrary Loan: An Acceptable Alternative to Purchase." *Wilson Library Bulletin* 63(5): 54–56.

Mellendorf, Scott A. 1993. "A Practical Method for Using Interloan Data to Assist Librarians with Collection Development." *OCLC Systems & Services* 9(2): 45–48.

Miller, Ruth. 1996. "Collection Management and Interlibrary Loan: Improving the Access/ownership Balance." *Journal of the Hong Kong Library Association* 18: 41–48.

Mortimore, Jeffrey M. 2006. "Access-informed Collection Development and the Academic Library: Using Holdings, Circulation, and ILL Data to Develop Prescient Collections." *Collection Management* 30(3): 21–37.

Murphy, Molly and Karen Rupp-Serrano. 1999. "Interlibrary Loan and Document Delivery: Lessons to Be Learned." *Journal of Library Administration* 28(2): 15–24.

New, Doris E, and Retha Zane Ott. 1974. "Interlibrary Loan Analysis As a Collection Development Tool." *Library Resources & Technical Services* 18(3): 275–83.

Nixon, Judith M., Freeman, Robert S. and Ward, Suzanne M. 2010. "Patron-driven Acquisitions: An Introduction and Literature Review." *Collection Management* 35(3/4): 119–24.

———. and E. Stewart Saunders. 2010. "A Study of Circulation Statistics of Books on Demand: A Decade of Patron-driven Collection Development, Part 3." *Collection Management* 35(3/4): 151–61.

Oberlander, Cyril and Mary Oberlander. 2004. "Resource Sharing Data: Mining for Selection and Meaning in Collection Development." *Against the Grain* 16(4): 77–81.

Ochola, John N. 2002. "Use of Circulation Statistics and Interlibrary Loan Data in Collection Management." *Collection Management* 27(1): 1–13.

Perdue, Jennifer and James A. Van Fleet. 1999. "Borrow or Buy? Cost-effective Delivery of Monographs." *Journal of Interlibrary Loan, Document Delivery & Information Supply* 9(4): 19–28.

Pitcher, Kate, Tim Bowersox, Cyril Oberlander, and Mark Sullivan. 2010. "Point-of-need Collection Development: The Getting It System Toolkit (GIST) and a New System for Acquisitions and Interlibrary Loan Integrated Workflow and Collection Development." *Collection Management* 35(3/4): 2, 22–36.

Polanka, Sue (ed). 2011. *No Shelf Required: E-Books in Libraries.* Chicago: American Library Association.

———. 2012. *No Shelf Required 2: Use and Management of Electronic Books.* Chicago: American Library Association.

———. 2009. "Patron-driven Acquisition." *Booklist* 105(9/10): 121.

Poremba, Sue Marquette. 2008. "Take a Look at Today's Vibrant Ebook Market." *EContent* 31(2): 32–37.

Price, Jason, and John McDonald. *Beguiled by Bananas? A Retrospective Study of Usage and Breadth of Patron- vs. Librarian-acquired Ebook Collections: Presentation on Ebook Acquisition at Academic Libraries given at XXIX Annual Charleston Conference: Issues in Book and Serial Acquisition,* November 5, 2009. http://ccdl.libraries.claremont.edu/cdm4/item_viewer.php?CISOROOT=/lea&CISOPTR=177 (accessed April 23, 2012).

Pritchard, S. J. 1980. "Purchase and Use of Monographs Originally Requested on Interlibrary Loan in a Medical School Library." *Library Acquisitions: Practice and Theory* 4(2): 135–39.

Reighart, Renee and Cyril Oberlander. 2008. "Exploring the Future of Interlibrary Loan: Generalizing the Experience of the University of Virginia, USA." *Interlending & Document Supply* 36(4): 184–90.

Reed, Catherine A. 2004. "Expanding the ILL Role: Interlibrary Loan Contributing to Collection Development." *Against the Grain* 16(4): 44, 46, 49.

Rottmann, F. K. 1991. "To Buy or to Borrow: Studies of the Impact of Interlibrary Loan on Collection Development in the Academic Library." *Journal of Interlibrary Loan & Information Supply* 1(3): 17–27.

Reynolds, Leslie J., Carmelita Pickett, Wyoma vanDuinkerken, Jane Smith, Jeanne Harrell, and Sandra Tucker. 2010. "User-driven Acquisitions: Allowing Patron Requests to Drive Collection Development in an Academic Library." *Collection Management* 35(3/4): 244–54.

Roberts, Michael, and Kenneth J. Cameron. 1984. "A Barometer of Unmet Demand: Interlibrary Loans Analysis and Monographic Acquisitions." *Library Acquisitions: Practice and Theory* 8(1): 31–42.

Rosen, Judith. 2010. "BookPrep: POD in the Cloud." *Publisher's Weekly* 257 (10): 6, 8.

Ruppel, Margie. 2006. "Tying Collection Development's Loose Ends with Interlibrary Loan." *Collection Building* 25(3): 72–77.

Schell, Lindsey. 2011. "The Academic Library E-Book." In *No Shelf Required*, ed. Sue Polanka. Chicago: American Library Association, 75–87.

Silva, Erin S. and Cherié L. Weible. 2010. "Own Not Loan: Different Request Sources for Purchase Lists." *Collection Management* 35(3/4): 180–84.

Squires, Lucy and Sue Laurence. "I Feel More into Reading:" Gloucestershire's 'Children Selecting Books' Project." *School Librarian* 50(2): 68–69, 71.

Swanson, Ann. 1985. "Using Interlibrary Loan as a Factor in Collection Development." *The Unabashed Librarian* 56: 15–16.

Tenopir, Carol. 2010. "New Directions for Collections." *Library Journal* 135(10): 24.

Trueswell, Richard L. 1969. "Some Behavioral Patterns of Library Users: The 80/20 Rule." *Wilson Library Bulletin* 43(5): 458–61.

Tyler, David C., Yang Xu, Joyce C. Melvin, Marylou Epp, and Anita M. Kreps. 2010. "Just How Right Are the Customers? An Analysis of the Relative Performance of Patron-initiated Interlibrary Loan Monograph Purchases." *Collection Management* 35(3/4): 162–79.

Walters, William H. 2012. "Patron-Driven Acquisitions and the Educational Mission of the Academic Library." *Library Resources and Technical Services* 56(3): 199-213.

Ward, Suzanne M. 2002. "Books on Demand: Just-in-time Acquisitions." *Acquisitions Librarian* 27: 95–107.

———., Tanner Wray, and Karl E. Debus-López. 2003. "Collection Development Based on Patron Requests: Collaboration between Interlibrary Loan and Acquisitions." *Library Collections, Acquisitions, and Technical Services* 27(2): 203–13.

Watson, Paula D. 2004. "E-publishing Impact on Acquisitions and Interlibrary Loan: E-publishing: A Rapidly Maturing Industry. *Library Technology Reports* 40(6): 5–76.

Wessling, Julie E. 1989. "Benefits from Automated IL Borrowing Records: Use of ILLRKS in an Academic Library." *RQ* 29(Winter): 209–18.

Wood, David N. and Cathryn A. Bower. 1969. "Survey of Medical Literature Borrowed from the National Lending Library for Science and Technology." *Bulletin of the Medical Library Association* 57(1): 47.

Zopfi-Jordan, David. 2008. Purchasing or Borrowing: Making Interlibrary Loan Decisions That Enhance Patron Satisfaction. *Journal of Interlibrary Loan, Document Delivery & Electronic Reserve* 18(3): 387–94.

reference notes

1. Suzanne M. Ward, Tanner Wray, and Karl E. Debus-López, "Collection Development Based on Patron Requests: Collaboration between Interlibrary Loan and Acquisitions," *Library Collections, Acquisitions, and Technical Services* 27, no. 2 (2003): 203–13.

2. Ann Swanson, "Using Interlibrary Loan as a Factor in Collection Development," *The Unabashed Librarian* 56 (1985): 15–16; Megan Allen, Suzanne M. Ward, Tanner Wray, and Karl E. Debus-López, "Patron-Focused Services: Cooperative Interlibrary Loan, Collection Development And Acquisitions," *Interlending & Document Supply* 30, no. 2 (2003): 138–41; Sharon A. Campbell, "To Buy or to Borrow, That Is the Question," *Journal of Interlibrary Loan, Document Supply and Electronic Reserve* 16, no. 3 (2006):35–39; Richard Hulsey, "Purchase on Demand: A Better Customer Service Model," *Library Journal* 128, no.10 (2003): 77; Terry Mackey, "Interlibrary Loan: An Acceptable Alternative to Purchase," *Wilson Library Bulletin* 63, no.5 (1989): 54–56.

3. Lucy Squires and Sue Laurence, "'I Feel More into Reading:' Gloucestershire's Children Selecting Books' Project," *School Librarian* 50, no. 2 (2002): 68–69, 71.

4. G. G. Allen, "The Economic Efficiencies of Alternatives to Purchase and Loan of Library Resources," *IATUL Quarterly* 2, no. 4(1988): 209–14; Robert N. Broadus, "Use Studies of Library Collections," *Library Resources & Technical Services* 24, no. 4 (1980): 317–24; Larry Hardesty, "Use of Library Materials at a Small Liberal Arts College," *Library Research* 3, no. 3 (1981): 261–82; Allen Kent, *Use of Library Materials: The University of Pittsburgh Study,* (New York: M. Dekker, 1979); Richard L. Trueswell, "Some Behavioral Patterns of Library Users: The 80/20 Rule," *Wilson Library Bulletin* 43, no. 5(1969): 458–61.

5. Chris Anderson, *The Long Tail: Why the Future of Business Is Selling Less of More,* (New York: Hyperion, 2006).

6. Martha Kyrillidou and Les Bland, eds., *ARL Statistics 2007–2008,* (Washington, D.C.: Association of Research Libraries, 2009).

7. Laura Townsend Kane, "Access vs. Ownership: Do We Have to Make a Choice?" *College & Research Libraries* 58, no. 1 (1997): 59–67.

8. Kate Pitcher, Tim Bowersox, Cyril Oberlander, and Mark Sullivan, "Point-of-Need Collection Development: The Getting It System Toolkit (GIST) and a New System for Acquisitions and Interlibrary Loan Integrated Workflow and Collection Development," *Collection Management* 35, nos. 3/4 (2010):222–36.

9. Michael Roberts and Kenneth J. Cameron, "A Barometer of Unmet Demand: Interlibrary Loans Analysis and Monographic Acquisitions," *Library Acquisitions: Practice and Theory* 8, no. 1 (1984): 31–42.

10. Laura M. Bartolo, "Automated ILL Analysis and Collection Development: A Hi-Tech Marriage of Convenience," *Library Acquisitions: Practice and Theory* 13, no. 4 (1989): 361–69; Barbara Beaton and Jay H. Kirk, "Application of an Automated Interlibrary Loan Log," *Journal of Academic Librarianship* 14, no. 1 (1988): 24–27; Gary D. Byrd, D. A. Thomas, and Katherine E. Hughes, "Collection Development Using Interlibrary Loan Borrowing and Acquisitions Statistics," *Bulletin of the Medical Library Association* 70, no. 1 (1982): 1–9; Mary E. Jackson, "Library to Library," *Wilson Library Bulletin* 64, no. 4 (1989): 88–89; Mounir A. Khalil, "Applications of an Automated ILL Statistical Analysis as a Collection Development Tool," *Journal of Interlibrary Loan, Document Delivery & Information Supply* 4, no. 1 (1993): 45–54; Jennifer E. Knievel, Heather Wicht, and Lynn Silipigni Connaway, "Use of Circulation Statistics and Interlibrary Loan Data in Collection Management," *College & Research Libraries* 67, no. 1 (2006): 35; Jo Ann Lahmon, "Using Interlibrary Loan Data in Collection Development" *OCLC Micro* 7, no. 5 (1991): 19–22; Barbara Lockett, ed., *Guide to the Evaluation of Library Collections*, (Chicago: American Library Association, 1989); Scott A. Mellendorf, "A Practical Method for Using Interloan Data to Assist Librarians with Collection Development," *OCLC Systems & Services* 9, no. 2 (1993): 45–48; Jeffrey M. Mortimore, "Access-Informed Collection Development and the Academic Library: Using Holdings, Circulation, and ILL Data to Develop Prescient Collections," *Collection Management* 30, no. 3 (2006): 21–37; Molly Murphy and Karen Rupp-Serrano, "Interlibrary Loan and Document Delivery: Lessons to Be Learned," *Journal of Library Administration* 28, no. 2 (1999): 15–24; Doris E. New and Retha Zane Ott, "Interlibrary Loan Analysis as a Collection Development Tool," *Library Resources & Technical Services* 18, no. 3 (1974): 275–83; Cyril Oberlander and Mary Oberlander, "Resource Sharing Data: Mining for Selection and Meaning in Collection Development," *Against the Grain* 16, no. 4 (2004): 77–81; John N. Ochola, "Use of Circulation Statistics and Interlibrary Loan Data in Collection Management," *Collection Management* 27, no. 1 (2002): 1–13; S. J. Pritchard, "Purchase and Use of Monographs Originally Requested on Interlibrary Loan in a Medical School Library," *Library Acquisitions: Practice and Theory* 4, no. 2 (1980): 135–39; Roberts and Cameron, "A Barometer of Unmet Demand"; Julie E. Wessling, "Benefits from Automated IL Borrowing Records: Use of ILLRKS in an Academic Library," *RQ* 29 (Winter 1989): 209–18.

11. Pritchard, "Purchase and Use of Monographs."

12. Swanson, "Using Interlibrary Loan as a Factor in Collection Development."

13. Allen, "The Economic Efficiencies."

14. Anna Herslow-Fex, "Interlibrary Loan Statistics: An Instrument for Collection Development," *LIBER Bulletin* 34 (1989): 73–75.

15. Ruth Miller, "Collection Management and Interlibrary Loan: Improving the Access/Ownership Balance," *Journal of the Hong Kong Library Association* 18 (1996): 41–48.

16. Murphy and Rupp-Serrano, "Interlibrary Loan and Document Delivery."

17. Jennifer Perdue and James A. Van Fleet, "Borrow or Buy? Cost-Effective Delivery of Monographs," *Journal of Interlibrary Loan, Document Delivery & Information Supply* 9, no. 4 (1999): 19–28.

18. Bartolo, "Automated ILL Analysis and Collection Development"; Camille Livingston and Antje Mays, "Using Interlibrary Loan Data as a Selection Tool: ILL Trails Provide Collection Clues," *Against the Grain* 16, no. 2 (2004): 22–28; Roberts and Cameron, "A Barometer of Unmet Demand."

19. Mary E. Jackson, *Measuring the Performance of Interlibrary Loan Operations in North American Research & College Libraries* (Washington, D.C.: Association of Research Libraries, 1998).

20. Suzanne M. Ward, "Books on Demand: Just-in-Time Acquisitions," *Acquisitions Librarian* 27 (2002): 95–107; Ward, et al., "Collection Development Based on Patron Requests"; Allen, et al., "Patron-focused Services."

21. Nancy Lichten Alder, "Direct Purchasing as a Function of Interlibrary Loan: Buying Books Versus Borrowing," *Journal of Interlibrary Loan, Document Delivery & Electronic Reserve* 18, no. 1 (2007): 9–15; Barbara M. Coopey and Ann M. Snowman, "ATG Special Report: ILL Purchase Express," *Against the Grain* 18, no. 1 (2006): 46–49; Erin S. Silva and Cherié L. Weible, "Own Not Loan: Different Request Sources for Purchase Lists," *Collection Management* 35, nos. 3/4 (2010): 180–84; Ward, et al., "Collection Development Based on Patron Requests."

22. Silva and Weible, "Own Not Loan."

23. Louis Houle, "Convergence between Interlibrary Loan and Acquisitions: A Science and Engineering Library Experience," *IATUL Proceedings* 14 (2004): 1–7.

24. David Zopfi-Jordan, "Purchasing or Borrowing: Making Interlibrary Loan Decisions That Enhance Patron Satisfaction," *Journal of Interlibrary Loan, Document Delivery & Electronic Reserve* 18, no. 3 (2008): 387–94.

25. Hulsey, "Purchase on Demand."

26. Houle, "Convergence between Interlibrary Loan and Acquisitions."

27. Alder, "Direct Purchasing as a Function of Interlibrary Loan."

28. Judith M. Nixon and E. Stewart Saunders, "A Study of Circulation Statistics of Books on Demand: A Decade of Patron-Driven Collection Development, Part 3," *Collection Management* 35, nos. 3/4 (2010): 151–61.

29. Marianne Stowell Bracke, "Science and Technology Books on Demand: A Decade of Patron-Driven Collection Development, Part 2," *Collection Management* 35, nos. 3/4 (2010): 142–50; Nixon and Saunders, "A Study of Circulation Statistics of Books on Demand."

30. Michelle Foss, "Books-On-Demand Pilot Program: An Innovative 'Patroncentric' Approach to Enhance the Library Collection," *Journal of Access Services* 5, nos. 1/2 (2007): 306–15.

31. Renee Reighart and Cyril Oberlander, "Exploring the Future of Interlibrary Loan: Generalizing the Experience of the University of Virginia, USA," *Interlending & Document Supply* 36, no. 4 (2008): 184–90.

32. Ward, "Books on Demand."

33. Kristine J. Anderson, Robert S. Freeman, Jean-Pierre V. M. Hérubel, Lawrence J. Mykytiuk, Judith M. Nixon, and Suzanne M. Ward, "Liberal Arts Books on Demand: A Decade of Patron-Driven Collection Development, Part 1," *Collection Management* 35, nos. 3/4 (2010): 125–41 and David C. Tyler, Yang Xu, Joyce C. Melvin, Marylou Epp, and Anita M. Kreps, "Just How Right Are the Customers? An Analysis of the Relative Performance of Patron-Initiated Interlibrary Loan Monograph Purchases," *Collection Management* 35, nos. 3/4 (2010): 162–79.

34. Madeleine Bombeld and Arlene Hanerfeld, "The Surprising Truth about Faculty Perception and Use of Collection Development Opportunities: One Library's Case Study," *Against the Grain* 16, no. 2 (2004): 18, 20, 22; Sandy Brug and Cristi MacWaters, "Patron-Driven Purchasing from Interlibrary Loan Requests," *Colorado Libraries* 30, no. 3 (2004): 36–38; Gayle Rosemary Y. C. Chan, "Purchase Instead of Borrow: An International Perspective," *Journal of Interlibrary Loan Document Delivery and Information Supply* 14, no. 4 (2004): 23–37; Alberta Comer and Elizabeth A. Lorenzen, "Biz of Acq: Is Purchase-on-Demand a Worthy Model? Do Patrons Really Know What They Want?" *Against the Grain* 17, no. 1 (2005): 75–78; Campbell "To Buy or to Borrow"; Houle, "Convergence between Interlibrary Loan and Acquisitions"; Uta Hussong-Christian and Kerri Goergen-Doll, "We're Listening: Using Patron Feedback to Assess and Enhance Purchase on Demand," *Journal of Interlibrary Loan, Document Delivery & Electronic Reserve* 20, no. 5 (2010): 319–35.

35. Foss, "Books-On-Demand Pilot Program."

36. Hussong-Christian and Goergen-Doll, "We're Listening."

37. Ward, "Books on Demand"; Anderson, et al., "Liberal Arts Books on Demand."

38. Hussong-Christian and Goergen-Doll, "We're Listening."

39. Alder, "Direct Purchasing as a Function of Interlibrary Loan."

40. Anderson et al., "Liberal Arts Books on Demand"; Bracke, "Science and Technology Books on Demand"; Nixon and Saunders, "A Study of Circulation Statistics of Books on Demand"; Tyler et al., "Just How Right Are the Customers?"

41. Coopey and Snowman, "ATG Special Report"; Catherine A. Reed, "Expanding the ILL Role: Interlibrary Loan Contributing to Collection Development," *Against the Grain* 16, no. 4 (2004): 44, 46, 49; Margie Ruppel, "Tying Collection Development's Loose Ends with Interlibrary Loan," *Collection Building* 25, no. 3 (2006): 72–77; Ward, "Books on Demand."

42. Ruppel, "Tying Collection Development's Loose Ends."

43. Ward, et al., "Collection Development Based on Patron Requests."

44. Silva and Weible, "Own Not Loan."

45. Brug and MacWaters, "Patron-Driven Purchasing from Interlibrary Loan Requests."

46. Catherine Anson and Ruth R. Connell, *E-Book Collections, SPEC Kit no. 313* (Washington, D.C.: Association of Research Libraries, 2009).

47. Dracine Hodges, Cyndi Preston, and Marsha J. Hamilton, "Resolving the Challenge of E-Books," *Collection Management* 35, nos. 3/4 (2010): 196–200; Sue Polanka, ed., *No Shelf Required: E-Books in Libraries* (Chicago: American Library Association, 2011); Sue Polanka, ed., *No Shelf Required 2: Use and Management of Electronic Books* (Chicago: American Library Association, 2012).

48. Pitcher, et al., "Point-of-Need Collection Development."

49. Sue Polanka, "Patron-driven Acquisition," *Booklist* 105, nos. 9/10 (2009): 121.

50. Diane Carroll, "Ebooks: Taking the Next Step," 2010 https://research.wsulibs .wsu.edu:8443/jspui/bitstream/2376/2568/1/EBooks%20Taking%20the% 20next%20step%20Timberline%20May%202010.pdf (accessed April 23, 2012).

51. Dracine Hodges, Cyndi Preston, and Marsha J. Hamilton, "Patron-Initiated Collection Development: Progress of a Paradigm Shift," *Collection Management* 35, nos. 3/4 (2010): 208–21.

52. Lindsey Schell, "The Academic Library E-Book," in *No Shelf Required,* ed. by Sue Polanka, (Chicago: American Library Association, 2011), 75–87.

53. Carol Tenopir, "New Directions for Collections," *Library Journal* 135, no. 10 (2010): 24.

54. Pitcher et al., "Point-of-Need Collection Development"; Leslie J. Reynolds, Carmelita Pickett, Wyoma vanDuinkerken, Jane Smith, Jeanne Harrell, and Sandra Tucker, "User-Driven Acquisitions: Allowing Patron Requests to Drive Collection Development in an Academic Library," *Collection Management* 35, nos. 3/4 (2010): 244–54.

55. Hodges et al., "Patron-Initiated Collection Development."

56. Jason Price and John McDonald, *Beguiled by Bananas? A Retrospective Study of Usage and Breadth of Patron- vs. Librarian-Acquired Ebook Collections: Presentation on E-Book Acquisition at Academic Libraries Given at XXIX Annual Charleston Conference: Issues in Book and Serial Acquisition,* November 5, 2009. http://ccdl.libraries.claremont.edu/cdm4/item_viewer.php?CISOROOT=/lea &CISOPTR=177(accessed April 23, 2012).

57. Pitcher et al., "Point-of-Need Collection Development"

58. Reynolds et al., "User-Driven Acquisitions."

59. Anne C. Barnhart, "Want Buy-In? Let Your Students Do the Buying! A Case Study of Course-Integrated Collection Development," *Collection Management* 35, nos. 3/4 (2010): 237–43.

60. Squires and Laurence, "'I Feel More into Reading.'"

61. Michael R. Colford, "Rethinking Resource Sharing: Boston Public Library Provides Scan-on-Demand for Interlibrary Loan," *Interface* 30, no. 1 (2008): 5–6.

62. William C. Dougherty,. "Print on Demand: What Librarians Should Know," *Journal of Academic Librarianship* 35, no.2 (2009): 184–86 and Barbara Blummer, "Opportunities for Libraries with Print-on-Demand Publishing," *Journal of Access Services* 3, no. 2 (2005): 41–54.

63. Judith Rosen, "BookPrep: POD in the Cloud," *Publisher's Weekly* 257, no. 10 (2010): 6, 8.

64. Kathleen Carlisle Fountain and Linda Frederiksen, "Just Passing through: Patron-Initiated Collection Development in Northwest Academic Libraries," *Collection Management* 5, nos. 3/4 (2010): 185–95.

65. Nixon and Saunders, "A Study of Circulation Statistics of Books on Demand"; Tyler et al., "Just How Right Are the Customers?"

66. Tenopir, "New Directions for Collections."

67. Ward, et al., "Collection Development Based on Patron Requests."

68. Houle, "Convergence between Interlibrary Loan and Acquisitions."

69. Hussong-Christian and Goergen-Doll, "We're Listening."

70. Jane L. Ingold, "Buyer Beware: Using Interlibrary Loan Requests in Purchasing Decisions," *Against the Grain* 16, no. 2 (2004): 30, 32, 34.

71. Hodges et al., "Patron-Initiated Collection Development"; Polanka, "Patron-Driven Acquisition."

72. Marianne Stowell Bracke, Jean-Pierre V. M. Hérubel, and Suzanne M. Ward, "Some Thoughts on Opportunities for Collection Development Librarians," *Collection Management* 35, nos. 3/4 (2010): 255–59.

73. Michael Levine-Clark, "Developing a Multiformat Demand-Driven Acquisition Model," *Collection Management* 35, nos. 3/4 (2010): 201–207.

74. Bracke et al., "Some Thoughts on Opportunities for Collection Development Librarians."

75. Joe Badics, "Acquisitions and Interlibrary Loan Together: Good Marriage or Will George W. Bush Object?" *Against the Grain* 16, no. 4 (2004): 52, 54; Pitcher et al., "Point-of-Need Collection Development."

about the author

SUZANNE M. WARD is Head, Collection Management at the Purdue University Libraries. She served as Head, Access Services from 1993 to 2009. In this role, Ward was instrumental in establishing the Purdue University Libraries' Books on Demand program in 2000, one of the pioneering interlibrary loan book purchase programs. In her current position, she coordinates entry into an e-book PDA plan.

CPSIA information can be obtained at www.ICGtesting.com
Printed in the USA
LVOW100516101012

302204LV00001B/5/P

9 780838 986080